laboratory exercises in astronomy

Joseph R. Holzinger | Michael A. Seeds

Franklin and Marshall College, Lancaster, Pennsylvania

laboratory exercises in
astronomy

macmillan publishing co., inc.
New York
collier macmillan publishers
London

Macmillan Publishing Co., Inc.
866 Third Avenue, New York, New York 10022

Collier Macmillan Canada, Ltd.

PRINTING   12 13 14 15   YEAR   2 3 4 5

ISBN   0-02-356880-1

preface

The exercises in this manual cover a wide range of topics and expectations. Some are very easy; others are fairly difficult. The format used here should enable the instructor to select those exercises and parts of exercises that are most pertinent to his course.

A special effort has been made to involve students in observational activities through the construction of simple pieces of equipment such as the starfinder, pop-up celestial globe, coordinate grid, shadow stick board, sundial, and spectrum box. Other exercises involve the student in the use of observational data provided in this manual. In these exercises the student is expected to make measurements from photographs with a millimeter rule and then use this data to study some of the important principles and conclusions of modern astronomy. Access to a telescope will open other vistas, but elaborate equipment generally is not required for these exercises.

We have found that the level of mathematical sophistication in these exercises does not pose a forbidding problem to our liberal arts students. A minimum knowledge of trigonometry is needed only in Exercise 3 on the sundial and part of Exercise 11 on the shadow stick. Otherwise elementary high school algebra suffices for these exercises. Logarithms have been included to deal with problems of magnitude and distance. Many students can use logarithm tables or a calculator successfully, but we have provided an exercise on logarithms (Appendix C) to aid those who need a quick review or who are not familiar with the subject.

Two basic references, frequently mentioned throughout the manual, are *The Observer's Handbook,* John R. Percy, ed., The Royal Astronomical Society of Canada, 252 College Street, Toronto M5T 1R7, Canada (inexpensive), and *The American Ephemeris and Nautical Almanac,* U.S. Government Printing Office, Washington, D.C. 20402. In ordering these books the year should be specified. Instructors could ask each student to purchase an *Observer's Handbook* or simply provide two or three for class reference. A single copy of *The American Ephemeris and Nautical Almanac* would be sufficient.

Exercises 20 and 21 about the moon can be done with any lunar map that has astronomical coordinates and the names of features. We have found the *Sky and Telescope Lunar Map* to be ideal.

Although the exercises in this manual are not intended to be done in any specific order, it is possible to arrange some sequences by topic.

Time: 3, 6, 11, 12, 13
Coordinates: 1, 2, 6, 7, 8, 9, 10 (Appendix A)
Orbits of planets: 14, 15, 16, 17
Solar system: 16, 17, 18, 19, 20, 21, 22, 27
Observations with telescopes: 4, 5, 18, 19, 20
Distance determination: 16, 24, 31, 32, 33
Stellar astronomy: 23, 24, 29, 30, 31, 32, 34, 35, 36
Astrophysics: 25, 26, 27, 28, 29
Galactic structure: 35, 36, 37

The tear-out feature of this manual will enable instructors to check student progress regularly. Some of the exercises could be assigned as homework or as formal laboratory exercises. Others could be used as the basis of a term paper or as a project for an advanced student.

J. R. H.
M. A. S.

contents

unit III
the solar system

unit IV
stars

unit V
galaxies and cosmology

appendixes

list of illustrations for practical exercises

laboratory exercises in astronomy

unit I

instruments

exercise

1

the pop-up celestial globe

1 materials   Scissors, rubber cement, rubber band, *Observer's Handbook*.

2 purpose   The two halves of the pop-up globe can be assembled to form a foldable "globe" that can be used to study the appearance of the sky and the co-ordinates which are used to locate objects (see Figure 1–1).

3 assembly   The northern and southern hemispheres of your "globe" are printed on stiff paper (see Figures 1–2a and 1–2b on stiff paper on pages 277, 279). After the halves are cut out, use a ruler and a pointed instrument such as a nail to score the cardboard lightly on the dotted lines where it will be folded. Fold the globe and glue tab A to tab A. Continue to glue corresponding tabs together, then hook a 2-in. rubber band to one of the internal tabs and stretch it by means of a pencil so that it hooks over the opposite tab. You now have a "globe" that can be flattened and carried in a book until needed. You may wish to make small holes at the poles before assembling the globe so that it can be slipped onto a piece of wire (wire from a coathanger will do) which is then slipped onto a piece of styrofoam at an angle equal to your latitude. A small piece of tape wound around the wire at the South Pole will keep the globe in the desired position.

4 using the pop-up celestial globe

the evening sky

Your globe shows many of the constellations, eight nebulae (*) and the eclip-tic marked with dates to show the location of the Sun throughout the year.

3

Figure 1-1. Pop-up celestial globe.

activity

1. Estimate the right ascension and the declination of the Sun for the current date.

   Current date_____   R.A._____   Dec._____

2. With the polar axis of your globe elevated to your latitude and pointing north, turn the globe until the Sun is directly west. The globe will represent the appearance of the sky at sunset. Think of yourself as the observer looking at the sky from the center of this globe. As you rotate the globe clockwise on its axis you will see the changing sky throughout the night until sunrise.

4

(a) List the constellation(s) that will be directly overhead for the current date at the following times.

Sunset _____

Midnight _____

Sunrise _____

(b) Give the right ascension and the declination of the Sun at the following times:

Vernal equinox (March 21)   R.A. _____   Dec. _____

Summer solstice (June 21)   R.A. _____   Dec. _____

Autumnal equinox   R.A. _____   Dec. _____

Winter solstice   R.A. _____   Dec. _____

3. Halley's Comet will be bright in the winter of 1985–1986. Plot the positions of the comet as given below and note the dates on the globe.

Halley's Comet

Date	R.A.	Dec.
October 1, 1985	6^h12^m	$+20°30'$
November 15, 1985	3^h54^m	$+21°18'$
December 15, 1985	23^h13^m	$+ 3°48'$
February 15, 1986	20^h51^m	$-12°00'$
March 15, 1986	19^h58^m	$-22°48'$

(a) Would you find the comet in the evening sky or the morning sky on October 1, 1985? *Hint*: First plot the approximate position of the Sun on October 1. _____

(b) At about what time of the night will the comet rise on November 15, 1985? _____

(c) Estimate the direction and the altitude of the comet about an hour after sunset on December 15, 1985.

Direction _____   Altitude _____

(d) On the globe sketch the direction of the comet's tail on December 15, 1985 and February 15, 1986.

(e) Approximately when will the comet be nearest the Sun in the sky?

_____

world travel

Take a trip to the Earth's north pole by tipping the globe until the axis points straight up. The celestial equator and the celestial horizon now coincide.

activity

1. For what range of declinations of the Sun will the Sun remain above the horizon for 24 hours of the day? _____

2. For what range of declinations of the Sun will the Sun remain below the horizon for 24 hours of the day? _____
Now tip the globe until the axis is horizontal. This represents the appearance of the sky as it would be seen if you were on the Earth's equator. Turn the globe and observe that the Sun and stars rise and set vertically.

3. When does the Sun rise due east and set due west? _____

_____

the planets and moon

Use an *Observer's Handbook* or an *American Ephemeris and Nautical Almanac* to find the position of the planets and the Moon on your current date. Plot these positions on your globe.

activity

1. Which of these planets are to be found in the evening sky?

_____

2. Which are to be found in the morning sky? _____

_____

3. From your *Observer's Handbook* determine the date of a total eclipse of the Moon. Plot the positions of the Sun and Moon on this date. What do you conclude about the relative positions of the Sun and Moon at this time? _____

_____

exercise

3

design of a horizontal sundial

1 materials Straightedge, protractor, trigonometric tables, heavy cardboard.

2 purpose This exercise will enable you to construct a working horizontal sundial for your latitude. You may wish to refer to Exercise 12, Local Mean Time and Zone Time when using the sundial.

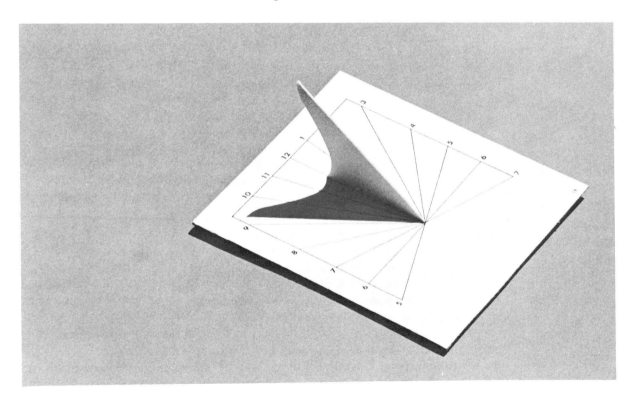

Figure 3-1. Horizontal sundial for latitude 40° N.

3 equation of time

The construction of a sundial (Figure 3-1) for a particular locality is dependent upon the latitude of the observer. A sundial constructed for a particular latitude will not indicate the correct apparent time for some other latitude.

For timekeeping purposes we invent a fictitious Sun, called the mean Sun, which moves at a uniform rate eastward along the celestial equator and goes from vernal equinox to vernal equinox in the same time it takes the apparent or true Sun moving at a nonuniform rate on the ecliptic to go from vernal equinox to vernal equinox. Apparent solar time, as kept by a sundial, may be defined as the local hour angle of the apparent Sun plus 12^h. The relation connecting apparent time with mean time is

$$\text{L.A.T.} - \text{L.M.T.} = \text{Eq.T.}$$

where L.A.T. is the local apparent time, L.M.T. is the local mean time, and Eq.T. is the equation of time.

Table 3-1   The Equation of Time in Minutes

Day	Jan.	Feb.	Mar.	Apr.	May	June	July	Aug.	Sept.	Oct.	Nov.	Dec.
1	−4	−14	−13	−4	3	2	−3	−6	0	10	16	11
4	−5	−14	−12	−3	3	2	−4	−6	1	11	16	10
7	−6	−14	−11	−2	3	2	−5	−6	2	12	16	9
10	−8	−14	−10	−1	4	1	−5	−5	3	13	16	7
13	−9	−14	−10	−1	4	0	−6	−5	4	14	16	6
16	−10	−14	−9	0	4	0	−6	−4	5	14	15	4
19	−11	−14	−8	1	4	−1	−6	−4	6	15	15	3
22	−12	−14	−7	1	4	−2	−6	−3	7	15	14	2
25	−12	−13	−6	2	3	−2	−6	−2	8	16	13	0
28	−13	−13	−5	2	3	−3	−6	−1	9	16	12	−2

The irregular rate of apparent solar time causes it to be alternately ahead of and behind mean time. The maximum difference is about 17^m. The days on which the two times are in agreement are April 15, June 15, September 1, and December 24. At these times Eq.T. = 0.

4 theory of a sundial

Examine Figure 3-2. The Sun, somewhere on the ecliptic (not shown), as it traces a diurnal circle during the course of a day, at some instant causes a stick or gnomon OA to cast a shadow OT on the plane of the celestial equator with an arc mT representing a time interval in degrees measured from noon. The corresponding arc NR in the plane of the observer's horizon represents the same time interval but will not have the same degree measure since equal arcs on the celestial equator do not project into equal arcs on the celestial horizon.

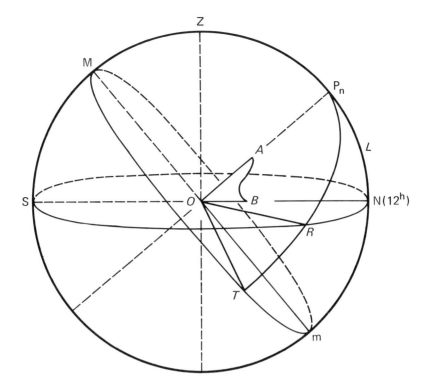

Mm : celestial equator
NS : celestial horizon
L   : latitude of observer or elevation of pole

Figure 3-2. Celestial sphere showing the relationships among the angles in the design of a horizontal sundial.

For example, if the observer's latitude were $40°$ and if the arc mT, numerically equal to $\angle mOT$, were $15°$ (1^h of time), the arc NR ($\angle NOR$), also representing 1^h of time, would only be $9° \, 46'$. This would represent the angle between 11^h and 12^h or 12^h and 1^h on the sundial face. It can be shown by spherical trigonometry that

$$\tan \angle NOR = \tan \angle mOT \sin L \qquad (3\text{--}1)$$

If $\angle mOT = 30°$, then $\angle NOR = 20° \, 22'$. This would mean that the angle between 10 o'clock and 12 o'clock or 12 o'clock and 2 o'clock would be $20° \, 22'$. Therefore the angle between 10 o'clock and 11 o'clock or the angle between 1 o'clock and 2 o'clock would be $10° \, 36'$ ($20° \, 22' - 9° 46'$).

5 design of a sundial

The sundial shown in Figure 3–3 has been designed for latitude $40°$ N. In this case we have taken $L = 40°$ and used equation (3–1) to calculate the angles NOR. A protractor was then used to draw the dial. The results of these calculations are given in Table 3–2.

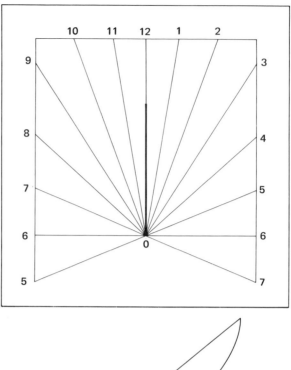

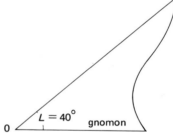

Figure 3-3. Sample layout of sundial for latitude 40° N. Observers in other latitudes must recompute hour marks and redraw gnomon.

Table 3-2 Angles calculated for 40° N

P.M. or A.M.	∡mOT	tan ∡mOT	sin L	tan ∡NOR	∡NOR
1 or 11	15°	.2679	.6428	.1722	9° 46′
2 or 10	30°	.5774	.6428	.3712	20° 22′
3 or 9	45°	1.0000	.6428	.6428	32° 44′
4 or 8	60°	1.7321	.6428	1.1134	48° 04′
5 or 7	75°	3.7321	.6428	2.3990	67° 22′
6 or 6	90°	∞	.6428	∞	90° 00′
7 or 5	105°	−3.7321	.6428	−2.3990	112° 38′

activity

Design and construct out of cardboard a sundial for your latitude. Mount the triangular gnomon, with base angle equal to your latitude, perpendicular to the sundial base on the 12 o'clock line. Begin by recording your latitude and longitude below and then complete Table 3–3.

Latitude _____   Longitude _____

Table 3-3 Angles for Construction of Sundial

P.M. or A.M.	∡mOT	tan ∡mOT	sin L	tan ∡NOR	∡NOR
1 or 11	15°	.2679			
2 or 10	30°	.5774			
3 or 9	45°	1.0000			
4 or 8	60°	1.7321			
5 or 7	75°	3.7321			
6 or 6	90°	∞			
7 or 5	105°	−3.7321			

6 orienting a sundial

When completed, the sundial should be set in a sunny spot and leveled. The gnomon or 12 o'clock line should point toward true north. This orientation may be accomplished in the following manner: Suppose the Z.T. is 10^h on September 25 and the observer is in longitude 76° 15′ W. Then the corresponding L.M.T. is 10^h minus 05^m, since we are 5^m west of the 75th or central meridian of zone 5. From Table 3–1 in Section 3 we find that Eq. T. = 8^m for the given date. Then L.A.T. = L.M.T. + Eq.T. or L.A.T. = 10^h 03^m corresponding to the given Z.T. and date. Turn the dial until the shadow cast by the gnomon shows approximately 10^h 03^m. The dial is now oriented along a true north-south line.

7 using a a sundial

In using the dial, after it has been leveled and oriented, read the dial time (L.A.T.). Now use the formula L.A.T. − L.M.T. = Eq.T. to obtain the L.M.T., which is the mean solar time for your particular meridian. Compute the number of minutes between your meridian and the central meridian of your time zone. If you are west of the central meridian, add this difference to the L.M.T. to get Z.T.; otherwise subtract this difference.

problems

1. On November 21 in longitude 76° 15′ W we place an upright stick in the ground and, when the shadow is due north, decide to go home for lunch. Assuming that our watch is correct and on standard time, what time would we leave?
2. Find the L.A.T. at a place in longitude 76° W at the instant the Z.T. is 20^h 17^m on May 1.
3. Your Z.T. is 14^h 30^m on July 4 in longitude 76° W. What is the corresponding sundial time?

design of a horizontal sundial

Name _____

exercise

4

Section _____ Date _____

aligning and using a 6-in. reflector telescope

1 **references and materials**

6-in. reflector telescope, flashlight, star charts on pages 287, 289, 291 *Observer's Handbook.*

2 **purpose**

This exercise will guide you in the adjustment and the use of an equatorially mounted telescope (Figure 4–1).

3 **introduction**

The mounting of an equatorial telescope has two axes at right angles to each other. When the telescope is aligned, the polar axis of the telescope will be parallel to the polar axis (axis of rotation) of the earth. The star Polaris will lie very close to this line. The telescope must be moved in an east-west direction about the polar axis if it is to track a star.

The declination axis permits the telescope to be moved in a north-south direction. For each axis there is a coordinate or setting circle. Attached to the polar axis of the telescope is the right ascension circle, sometimes referred to as the hour circle. The declination circle is attached to the declination axis. Use of these circles will enable you to locate various objects in the sky.

4 **aligning the polar axis**

The first step in the alignment procedure requires you to elevate the polar axis of your telescope to an angle numerically equal to your latitude. Unless you change your latitude this adjustment need only be done once and can be accomplished indoors with a devil level. Outdoors, turn the telescope tripod until the polar axis points at the star Polaris.

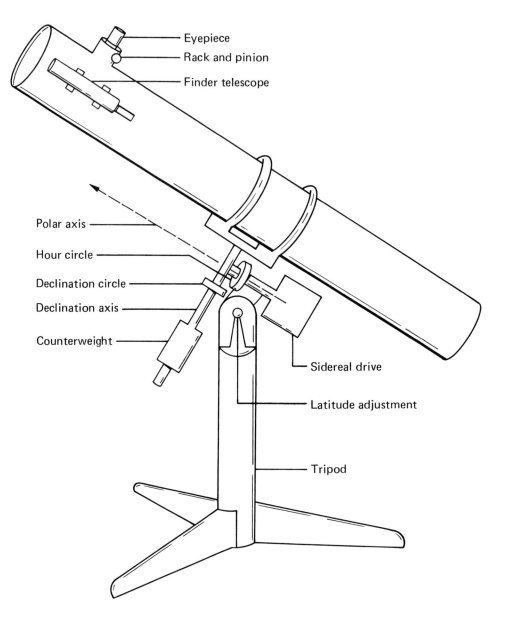

Figure 4-1. Principal parts of a typical 6-in. reflector telescope.

5 aligning the finder telescope with the main telescope

You will find a rack-and-pinion gear at the eyepiece of the telescope with which you can move the eyepiece in and out for focusing. It may be necessary also to move the eyepiece in and out of its cell to get a proper focus. A properly focused star should appear as a pinpoint of light, not as a ball or circle of light.

Should the finder be out of alignment, locate a bright star in the center of the field of the main telescope, then adjust the finder telescope until the star is also in the center of the field of view. Because the field of view of the finder is considerably larger than that of the main telescope, you will generally first locate the object you wish to observe in the center of the field of the finder, then turn your attention to the main telescope.

instruments

| 6 | adjusting the setting circles | Locate a known, bright star in the sky. Center it in the finder, then in the main telescope. Look up its right ascension (R.A.) and declination (Dec.) in the *Observer's Handbook* or estimate them from your star chart. |

Star_____   R.A._____   Dec._____

Now turn the hour circle dial which is on a slip ring (do not move the telescope itself) until the right ascension coordinate of the star is opposite the pointer. The declination of the star should appear opposite the pointer on the declination circle; if not, correct it. It is not necessary to adjust the declination circle once it is set correctly. Because of the rotation of the Earth you will need to keep moving the telescope about the polar axis from east to west to keep the object in the field of view.

| 7 | locating other objects | Now choose a second object and obtain its right ascension and declination from the *Observer's Handbook* or from your charts. *Just before you swing the telescope to the new object, check the hour circle and adjust it to read the correct right ascension for the object toward which the telescope is already pointed.* Now swing the telescope about the polar axis until the right ascension reading of this second object appears opposite the pointer on the hour circle. Move the telescope about the declination axis to the new declination. The object should now be in the field of view of the finder telescope. |

Each time you get ready to move to a new object adjust the hour circle just before you move the telescope. This makes it unnecessary for you to know the sidereal time or to have a sidereal drive mechanism on your telescope. If you are using a sidereal drive for tracking purposes, the use of the setting circles is the same.

activity

Locate and observe six of the objects listed below. Record the following:

Date_____ Latitude _____ Longitude _____ .

Object	Z.T.	R.A.	Dec.	Mag.	Description
Vega					
Arcturus					
Pleiades					
M42					
M13					
ε Lyrae					
Venus					
Mars					
Jupiter					
Saturn					
Moon					
Altair					
Rigel					

star charts for use at the telescope

1 materials

Telescope or mounted binoculars.

2 purpose

The charts in this exercise are intended to show you how to find your way about the sky with a telescope. They are also guides to some interesting objects in the sky. Two charts are included: Lyra and the Ring Nebula for summer and fall; Orion and the Great Nebula for the winter and early spring.

3 orientation of star charts

Most astronomical telescopes affect the field of view by making everything seem inverted and reversed. A few commercial telescopes and all binoculars have erect, unreversed fields of view. There are also some telescopes in which the field is right side up but reversed. You must decide which direction is north and which is east in your telescope's field of view. Locate a star and gently push the telescope tube southward. The star will move toward the north edge of the field. If you turn off the telescope drive or push the telescope tube to the east, the star will move toward the west and away from the east edge of the field.

The star charts in this exercise have the directions marked on them. If you keep in mind the orientation of your telescope's field of view and the directions on the chart, you should be able to find your way to some interesting stars.

4 Lyra and the Ring Nebula

Using the star charts following the appendices or a starfinder, locate the constellation of Lyra near Cygnus and the Milky Way. The brightest star, α Lyrae, also called Vega, is the second brightest star in the sky. Examine it through your telescope. Notice the effects of our atmosphere on the image. The light you see has traveled 26.5 light years from Vega, but the twinkling is caused by our atmosphere.

activity

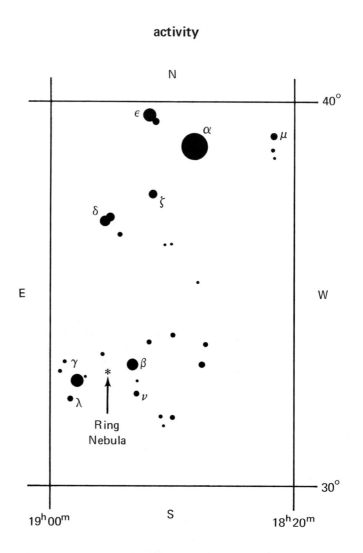

Figure 5-1. Finding chart for stars in the constellation Lyra.

1. Using the star chart shown in Figure 5–1, move your telescope to look at ε Lyrae. This star is called the "double double" because it is not a single star but rather two close binary systems separated by 207″ of arc. It is easy to see the two pairs as they are rather far apart, but the stars that make up each pair are very close together and may be difficult to resolve. Make a sketch of the position of the stars you see in the "double double."

instruments

2. Using the star chart in Figure 5–1, move your telescope to look at γ Lyrae or β Lyrae. The detailed map in Figure 5–2 shows an enlarged view of this area. Using Figure 5–2 move from the bright star to the fainter stars step by step until you come to the Ring Nebula. It is small and faint so you must work carefully to find it. Make a sketch of what you see.

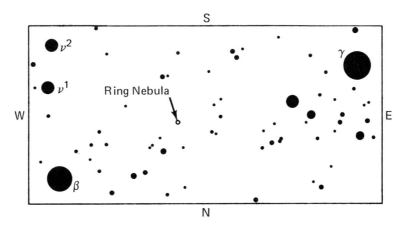

Figure 5-2. Detailed finding chart for the Ring Nebula in Lyra. Inverted for use at the telescope.

3. Look up the Ring Nebula in your text book and see if there is a good picture of it showing the central star. This central star is about 15th magnitude and may be visible in larger telescopes.

5 Orion and the Great Nebula

Using star charts or a starfinder, locate the constellation of Orion and identify α Orionis (Betelgeuse) and β Orionis (Rigel). Both of these stars are supergiants and are physically very large, but they differ in temperature. Compare the colors of the two stars. Betelgeuse, an M2 star, is quite cool and consequently appears reddish in color. Rigel is a hot star, a B8 star, and is blue-white in color.

Figure 5–3 shows the area of Orion's belt and sword. Compare this chart with the sky and locate the Great Nebula, M42, with your naked eye. Now locate the nebula with your telescope. Notice the complex filaments of nebulosity surrounding the stars at the center. These filaments can be traced throughout the constellation of Orion. The central bright portion of the nebula is a cloud of hydrogen, helium, nitrogen, oxygen, and other gases excited to fluorescence by the ultraviolet radiation of the hot stars imbedded

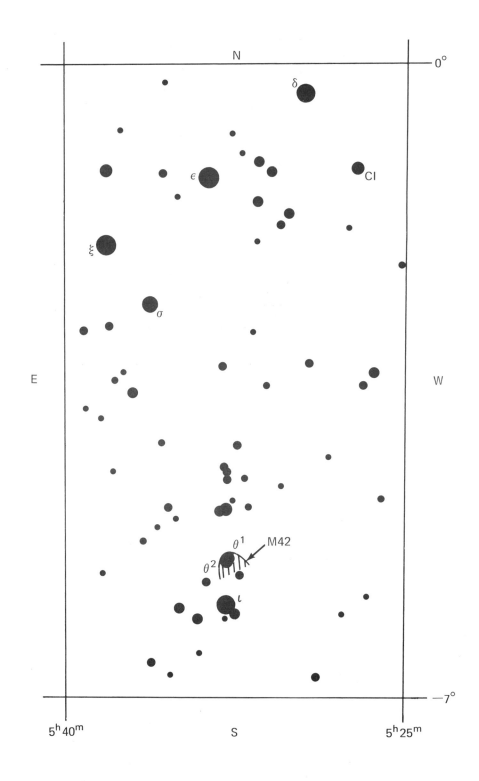

Figure 5-3. Finding chart for stars and nebulae in the belt and sword of Orion.

in the gas. The green tint of the nebula is produced by two spectral lines of oxygen in the green portion of the spectrum.

Make a careful sketch of the stars and filaments that you can see with your telescope.

Most of the constellation of Orion is filled with faint nebulosity. Move your telescope north from M42 to look at the next star up the sword. This star is also hot and a fainter nebula surrounds it.

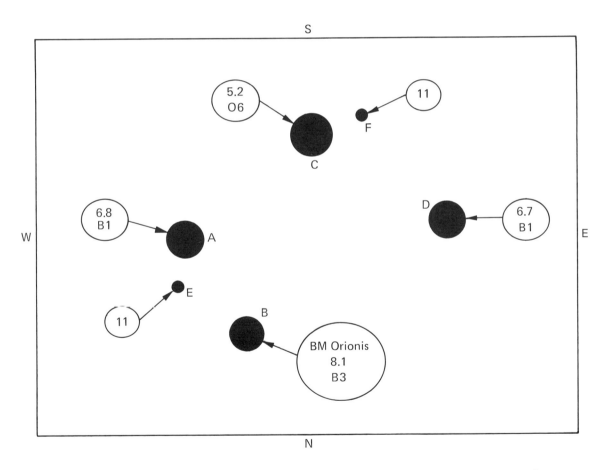

Figure 5-4. Detailed chart of the stars in the Great Nebula M42. Inverted for use at the telescope.

star charts for use at the telescope

Return to M42 and compare the small group of stars at the center of the nebula with the chart in Figure 5–4. These four stars are called the Trapezium, although their astronomical names are θ^1 Orionis A, B, C, and D. The magnitude and the spectral type of these are shown in Figure 5–4. Other stars have been found in this area including 11th magnitude stars E and F. These two stars are visible through a 6-in. telescope under good seeing conditions. Try to find them. Star B of the Trapezium is the eclipsing binary BM Orionis and has a period of about 6.5 days. The Trapezium stars are part of a small young cluster of a few hundred stars that are associated with M42. In fact most of the stars in the constellation of Orion are young, hot stars, and new stars are still being born out of the nebular material.

Examine the stars that make up the belt of Orion. These three bright stars are all blue stars. Consult Figure 5–3 and locate the star labeled CI Orionis. Compare the color of this star with that of the stars in the belt. This star is a K5 red giant and was catalogued as a variable star, but in fact its brightness has been shown to be constant. Its designation as a variable star is, therefore, a mistake.

unit II

coordinates and time

exercise

6

calculation of sidereal time

1 materials and references

American Ephemeris and Nautical Almanac, see Appendix A, page 263.

2 purpose

For an observer at a location for which the latitude and longitude are known, local sidereal time (L.S.T.) together with the equatorial coordinates of an object (right ascension and declination) are sufficient to determine the azimuth and altitude of the object. This exercise concerns itself with the calculation of L.S.T. by three methods.

3 conversion of arc into time

The Earth rotates through $360°$ in 24^h, therefore $15° = 1^h = 60^m$ or $1° = 4^m$. Table 6–1 gives the correspondence between arc units and time units.

Table 6–1

Arc Units	Time Units
$15°$	1^h
$1°$	4^m
$15'$	1^m
$1'$	4^s
$15''$	1^s

Example 6-1. $84°\ 47'\ 30'' = 5^h\ 39^m\ 10^s$

Solution	$75°$		$= 5^h$		
	$9°$			36^m	
		$45'$		03^m	
		$02'$			08^s
			$30''$		02^s
	$84°\ 47'\ 30'' = 5^h\ 39^m\ 10^s$				

4 **calculation of L.S.T. by table, first method (approximate)** Table 6-2 gives the approximate Greenwich Sidereal Time (G.S.T.) for 0^h G.M.T.

Table 6-2

Date		Hours	Minutes	Date		Hours	Minutes
Jan.	1	6	40	July	1	18	33
	15	7	35		15	19	29
Feb.	1	8	42	Aug.	1	20	36
	15	9	37		15	21	31
Mar.	1	10	32	Sept.	1	22	39
	15	11	28		15	23	34
Apr.	1	12	35	Oct.	1	0	37
	15	13	30		15	1	32
May	1	14	33	Nov.	1	2	39
	15	15	28		15	3	35
June	1	16	35	Dec.	1	4	38
	15	17	30		15	5	33

Because a sidereal clock gains nearly 4^m ($3^m\ 56^s$) daily over an ordinary clock, add 4^m for each day past the 1st or 15th of the month.

Example 6-2. What is the approximate L.S.T. in longitude 76° 15' W on April 4, 1975, when the zone time (Z.T.) is $22^h\ 00^m$ E.S.T.?

$$\lambda = 76°\ 15' = 5^h\ 05^m$$

For convenience we start with Z.T. $19^h\ 00^m$ on April 4. In order to get G.M.T. we first find the zone description (Z.D.) by dividing the longitude by 15 and rounding off to the nearest integer, then adding this integer (5 in this case) to the 19^h to get 0^h G.M.T. on April 5, 1975.

coordinates and time

The procedure is as follows:

Z.T.	$19^h\ 00^m$	Apr. 4, 1975
Z.D. for west longitude	$+\ 5^h$	
G.M.T.	$00^h\ 00^m$	Apr. 5, 1975
G.S.T. for Apr. 5 (from table)	$12^h\ 51^m$	
Correction for exact longitude (subtract)	$5^h\ 05^m$	
L.S.T. (corresponding to 19^h)	$7^h\ 46^m$	
Correction (approximate) $22^h - 19^h =$	3^h	
L.S.T. (corresponding to 22^h)	$10^h\ 46^m$	

Note: If the observer were in longitude 122° W on March 5, it would be appropriate to start with Z.T. $16^h\ 00^m$ because the zone description would be +8 and the G.M.T. $00^h\ 00^m$ on March 6.

If the observer were in longitude 43° E on March 5, it would be appropriate to start with Z. T. $03^h\ 00^m$ because the zone description would be -3 and the G.M.T. $00^h\ 00^m$ on March 5.

problems

1. Calculate the approximate L.S.T. for an observer in longitude 87° 30' W on May 7 when his Z.T. is $21^h\ 30^m$.

2. Calculate the approximate L.S.T. for an observer in longitude 33° 45' E on May 7 when his Z.T. is $01^h\ 30^m$.

5 approximate L.S.T. using September 21 date

On or about September 21 of any year, the sidereal clock and the ordinary clock are in agreement. Thereafter the sidereal clock gains approximately $3^m\ 56^s$ a day.

In the Example 6–2, April 4, 1975, is 195 days past September 21. Accordingly we add $12^h\ 47^m$ to $22^h\ 00^m$ and obtain $10^h\ 47^m$, which is the L.S.T. for the 75th meridian. Also, 76° 15' W is 5^m west of the central meridian, so we subtract 5^m from $10^h\ 47^m$ to obtain $10^h\ 42^m$, the approximate L.S.T. for the observer in longitude 76° 15' W.

problems

1. Calculate the approximate L.S.T. for an observer in longitude 87° 30' W on May 7 when his Z.T. is $21^h\ 30^m$.

2. Calculate the approximate L.S.T. for an observer in longitude 33° 45′ E on May 7 when his Z.T. is $01^h 30^m$.

6 L.S.T. precise to 1 second

In this method we use the table, Universal and Sidereal Times, 1975, found in *The American Ephemeris and Nautical Almanac* for that year. The following example illustrates the method:

Example 6-3. What is the L.S.T. for an observer in longitude 76° 15′ W on April 4, 1975, when the Z.T. is $22^h 00^m 00^s$ E.S.T.?

In the following Z.T. = zone time, Z.D. = zone description, G.M.T. = Greenwich mean time, λ = longitude, L.S.T. = local sidereal time, correction = time past 19^h. Note that the sidereal clock gains approximately 10^s per hour.

Z.T.	19^h	00^m	00^s	April 4, 1975
Z.D.	$+ 5^h$			
G.M.T.	00^h	00^m	00^s	April 5, 1975
G.S.T.	12^h	50^m	42^s	from *Ephemeris,* for 0^h G.M.T. April 5, (p. 14)
λ (w)	5^h	05^m	00^s	(subtract)
L.S.T.	7^h	45^m	42^s	for 19^h, April 4, 1975
Correction	3^h	00^m	30^s	time past 19^h plus gain of sidereal clock
L.S.T.	10^h	46^m	12^s	corresponding to $22^h 00^m$, April 4, 1975

Note: A method is given in *The American Ephemeris and Nautical Almanac* whereby L.S.T. may be calculated to a thousandth of a second.

problems

1. Calculate the L.S.T. for an observer in longitude 87° 30′ W on May 7, 1975 when his Z.T. is $21^h 30^m$.

2. Calculate the L.S.T. for an observer in longitude 33° 45′ E on May 7, 1975, when his Z.T. is $01^h 30^m$.

coordinates and time

instructions for constructing a starfinder

1 materials

A circular dial, declination dial and circle pointer are printed and included in this manual. Styrofoam sheets $\frac{3}{4}$ in. $\times$ 24 in. $\times$ 96 in. are inexpensive and may be purchased from a building supplies outlet as insulation. As many as a hundred starfinders may be made from one such piece. This material is easily cut on a bandsaw. White liquid glue is used throughout; rubber cement generally is not satisfactory. Circular levels are available from Sears or other mail order houses.

2 steps in assembling a starfinder

1. Cut out the circular dial in Figure 7–4 on page 281 and punch a $\frac{1}{4}$-in. hole at the center. Cut out the declination dial and punch a $\frac{1}{8}$-in. hole with a leather punch.

2. Cut from matte board or very heavy cardboard a base 5 in. $\times$ 3 in. and punch a $\frac{1}{4}$-in. hole for mounting on a tripod.

3. Cut from matte board a declination arm 5 in. $\times$ $\frac{3}{4}$ in. The declination scale is visible through a $\frac{3}{8}$-in hole. If a $\frac{3}{8}$-in. punch is not available, a square aperture $\frac{5}{16}$ in. $\times$ $\frac{5}{16}$ in. may be cut instead. Punch a $\frac{1}{8}$-in. hole to receive a 1 -in. long bolt, as shown in Figure 7–1.

4. Cut from $\frac{3}{4}$-in. styrofoam a rectangular piece about $3\frac{1}{4}$ in. $\times$ $2\frac{1}{4}$ in. using a bandsaw or jigsaw. Sand the edges of this piece by rubbing gently on a piece of sandpaper held flat on the table. To this piece glue the declination scale, as shown in Figures 7–1 and 7–3.

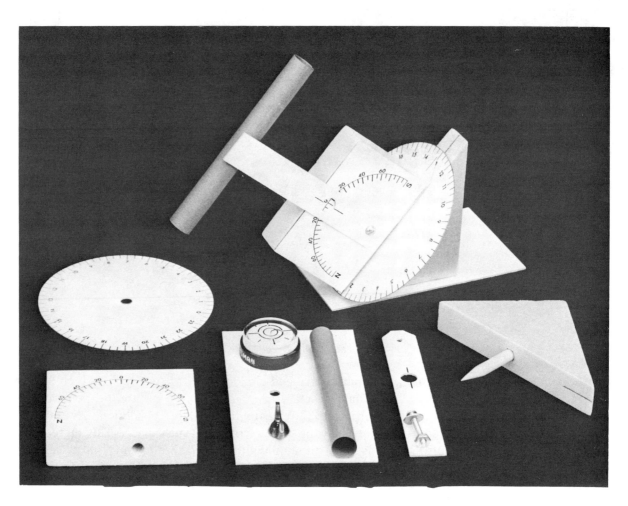

Figure 7-1. Starfinder parts and assembled instrument.

5. Cut from $\frac{3}{4}$-in. styrofoam a right triangular piece with base such that the hypotenuse is approximately $4\frac{3}{4}$ in. in length (see Figure 7–2). The upper angle (L) should be numerically equal to your latitude; the base angle then equals the complement of the latitude. At the upper vertex and centrally on the hypotenuse draw a line about 1 in. in length with a ballpoint pen.

6. Sharpen both ends of a 3-in. length of $\frac{1}{4}$-in. dowel stick.

7. On the hypotenuse and about $2\frac{3}{8}$ in. from the base of the triangular piece of styrofoam insert an end of the dowel stick. Insert the dowel stick by a slow twisting motion to about half its length while constantly viewing the stick from two angles to make certain that it is perpendicular to the hypotenuse.

coordinates and time

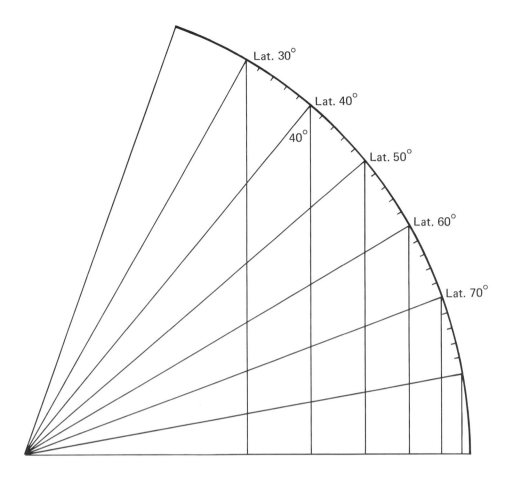

Figure 7-2. Template for determining the shape of the triangular piece of styrofoam according to latitude.

8. Remove the dowel stick from the triangular piece and insert it halfway into the bottom edge of the rectangular piece to which the declination dial has been glued, about $1\frac{1}{4}$ in. from the south end of the declination scale.

9. Remove the dowel stick from the declination block and glue it into the triangular block. About half the dowel stick should protrude from the hypotenuse of the triangular piece.

10. Roll a $4\frac{1}{2}$ in. $\times$ $4\frac{1}{2}$ in. piece of dark construction paper onto a length of $\frac{1}{2}$-in. dowel stick and glue. Hold until the glue sets, then slide it off the dowel stick. This is your viewing tube.

11. Use a nail to push a pilot hole through the rectangular piece of styrofoam at the point where the bolt holding the declination arm will pass.

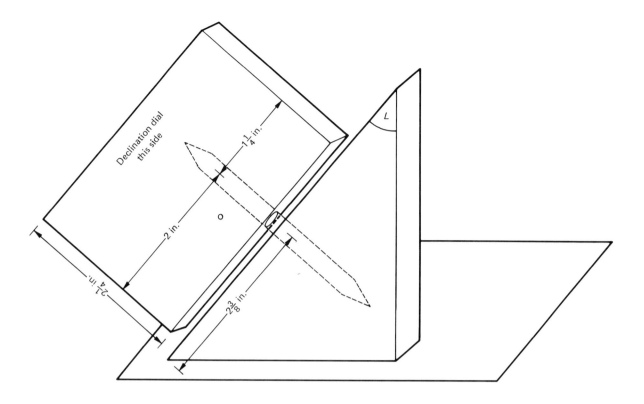

Figure 7-3. Position of pointed dowel stick in styrofoam pieces.

12. Insert the 1–in. bolt gently into the declination arm and then through the hole in the declination piece. Secure it with a washer and nut on the back and tighten it with your fingers.

13. Set the declination arm on 0°, turn the declination block over, and glue the viewing tube at right angles to the declination arm. A 2–in. wide spacer may be used to position and secure the viewing tube while the glue sets.

14. Glue the base of the triangular piece to the 5 in. ✕ 3 in. base, as seen in Figures 7–1 and 7–3. Remember that the latitude angle is up.

15. Glue the pointer to the base of the declination piece at the south end of the declination scale.

16. Place the declination block with attached declination arm and viewing tube on the dowel stick projecting from the triangular piece. Attach your starfinder to a photographer's tripod with a wingnut and level it with a circular level, which may be glued to the base of the starfinder or left loose as desired.

Directions for aligning and using the starfinder are included in Exercise 8 The Starfinder—Part I.

exercise

the starfinder—part I

8

1 materials Starfinder with circular level, tripod, *Observer's Handbook*, flashlight, see Appendix A and the star charts on pages 287, 289, 291.

2 purpose With a starfinder constructed for your latitude (the angle at the top of the right triangular block should be numerically equal to your latitude) and given the local sidereal time (L.S.T.) for your longitude, you will be able to determine a line of sight to any celestial object given its right ascension and declination. Also, you will be able to identify an "unknown" by sighting the object through the viewing tube, then reading its right ascension and declination from the dials. Reference to the table, The Brightest Stars (286 stars brighter than apparent magnitude 3.55), in *The Observer's Handbook* or to a star chart will enable you to identify the object if it is a star. (Other starfinder experiments are presented in Exercise 9, The Starfinder—Part II.)

3 determining sidereal time Approximate Greenwich sidereal time (G.S.T.) for 0^h Universal Time (G.M.T.) is shown in Table 8–1.

41

Table 8-1

Date		Hours	Minutes	Date		Hours	Minutes
Jan.	1	6	40	July	1	18	33
	15	7	35		15	19	29
Feb.	1	8	42	Aug.	1	20	36
	15	9	37		15	21	31
Mar.	1	10	32	Sept.	1	22	39
	15	11	28		15	23	34
Apr.	1	12	35	Oct.	1	0	37
	15	13	30		15	1	32
May	1	14	33	Nov.	1	2	39
	15	15	28		15	3	35
June	1	16	35	Dec.	1	4	38
	15	17	30		15	5	33

Because a sidereal clock gains nearly 4^m daily over an ordinary clock, add 4^m for each day past the 1st or 15th of the month.

Example 8-1. What is the approximate L.S.T. in longitude 76° 15′ W (5^h 05^m W) on April 4 when the zone time (Z.T.) is 22^h 00^m E.S.T.?

Z.T.	$19^h 00^m$	April 4
Z.D.*	5^h	
G.M.T.	$00^h 00^m$	April 5
G.S.T. (approximate) for Apr. 5 (from table)	$12^h 51^m$	
Correction for west longitude (subtract)	$5^h 05^m$	
L.S.T. (corresponding to 19^h)	$7^h 46^m$	
Correction (approximate) $22^h - 19^h =$	3^h	
L.S.T. (corresponding to 22^h)	$10^h 46^m$	

4 aligning the starfinder

Mount the starfinder on a tripod or base and adjust to a level position by use of a circular level. Compute the L.S.T. corresponding to your *standard time.* Set the sidereal time on the circular dial opposite the line drawn on the triangular block. Note that each small division on the dial represents 20^m of time.

Select a bright star that you know. Obtain its right ascension (R.A.) and declination (Dec.) from the list of brightest stars in *The Observer's Handbook* or from some other source such as a star chart, a celestial globe, or an ephemeris. A plus sign (or no sign) with the declination means *north* declination; a minus denotes *south* declination.

Set the right ascension of the star on the instrument by turning the pointer attached to the rectangular block to the appropriate figure on the circular

*To find zone description (Z.D.), divide the longitude by 15 and round off to the nearest whole number.

dial (the circular dial has already been set to the L.S.T.). Move the piece holding the viewing tube to the appropriate declination figure on the semi-circular dial.

Now turn the entire instrument (but not the tripod) until the star can be seen through the viewing tube. Lock the instrument in this position. The starfinder is now oriented, and you have a true north-south line. To locate other objects, set the sidereal time, the right ascension and declination of the object on the instrument. With a little practice, after the finder is oriented, it will take only a few seconds to locate an object.

Note: Bright objects appearing in the sky but which are not on the list of brightest stars are probably planets.

5 using the starfinder

Use the starfinder to locate six bright stars for which the coordinates are to be found in the table, The Brightest Stars, in *The Observer's Handbook*. Also use the starfinder to identify five unknown objects for which you determine the coordinates and then look for the identification in the list of brightest stars; these are listed in increasing order of right ascension.

The brightest stars have common names in addition to their scientific designations. For example, the brightest star in the constellation Lyra has the common name Vega; its scientific designation is Alpha Lyrae, abbreviated α Lyr. Faint stars may merely have number designations associated with the constellation name.

1. Align the starfinder, locate the first six objects, and complete the table by entering the date, Z.T., and corresponding sidereal time at the time of observation. Right ascension, declination, magnitude, and distance are given in *The Observer's Handbook*. In each case estimate the azimuth and altitude of the object at the time you view it. Indicate the scientific designation of the star, also its common name, if any. The vernal equinox and the north celestial pole are not objects, but you can furnish information concerning these celestial points.

2. Sight five other objects ("unknowns") in the sky with the starfinder. Set the L.S.T. and read the right ascension and declination from the appropriate dials. Use the list of brightest stars to identify these objects. If a bright object is not listed, it will probably be a planet. In this case refer to the planet diagrams in *The Observer's Handbook*. If a star you have selected is too faint to be included in the Handbook, use a star chart to identify the object.

Name _____

Section _____ Date _____

STARFINDER: FALL/SPRING

Date	Z.T.	L.S.T.	Object	R.A.	Dec.	Mag.	Distance	Azimuth	Altitude
			Vega (α Lyr.)	18^h 36.2^m	+38° 46'	0.04			
			Deneb ( )	20^h 40.7^m					
			Arcturus ( )						
			(η UMa)	13^h 46.8^m					
			Markab ( )	22^h 28.5^m	+58° 19'				
—	—	—	"Vernal Equinox"			—	—		
			Moon(Phase:)			—	—		
			"North Celestial Pole"						
			Capella (α Aur)	05^h 15.2^m	+45° 59'	0.05			
			Rigel ( )	05^h 13.6^m					
			Dubhe ( )						
			(α CMa)	06^h 44.2^m					
			Procyon ( )	05^h 35.2^m	−01° 13'				
—	—	—	"Vernal Equinox"			—	—		
			Moon(Phase:)			—	—		
			"North Celestial pole"						

F A L L

S P R I N G

44

9

the starfinder—part II

1 materials   Starfinder, tripod, flashlight, *Observer's Handbook*. For the special project, Section 6 of this exercise, you will also need the *American Ephemeris and Nautical Almanac* or tables for determining Greenwich sidereal time and a short wave radio or a watch set accurately to some known zone time. See Appendix A and the star charts on pages 287, 289, 291.

2 purpose   In this exercise you will use the starfinder to determine the local sidereal time (L.S.T.) from which it is possible to determine your zone time (Z.T.) or correct watch time. Approximate determination of right ascensions and declinations of visible objects may be effected with the starfinder. Finally you will see by way of an example how the starfinder may be used to determine latitude and longitude.

3 determina-tion of L.S.T. (Method 1)   Align your starfinder north-south by using Polaris. Pick a star that you recognize in the sky. Set its declination on the instrument and move the rectangular block until you can observe the star through the viewing tube. Now turn the circular dial until the right ascension (R.A.) of the star is under the cardboard pointer. Read the L.S.T. opposite the line on the triangular block.

activity

Record the following:

Star _____

R.A. _____   Longitude _____

Dec. _____   L.S.T. _____

Date _____   Time of observation _____

4 determination of L.S.T. (Method 2)

Align your starfinder north-south by using Polaris. If you observe, for example, a star that is due south (on the meridian), then, at this instant, L.S.T. = R.A. You have the right ascension of the star from your tables, hence you know the L.S.T.

This is the principle of the transit instrument such as is used by the U.S. Naval Observatory. They obtain L.S.T. in this way, then convert it to mean time. You can get the WWV Beltsville, Maryland, time signals on 2.5, 5, 10, 15, 20, 25 megacycles (MHz); CHU Ottawa, Canada signals on 3330, 7335, 14670 kilocycles (kHz).

Align the starfinder so that the observing tube is in the plane of the meridian and pointing south. Set the declination for a star that is slightly east of the meridian but which will transit the meridian shortly. When the star is in the center of the viewing tube, you may assume that it is on the meridian.

activity

Record the following when the star is on the meridian

Star _____

R.A. _____ Longitude _____

Dec. _____ L.S.T. _____

Date _____ Time of observation _____

problems

1. Draw a diagram illustrating that L.S.T. = R.A. when the star is on the meridian or due south.

2. Given the L.S.T. above, the date and your longitude, try to devise a method for finding the corresponding zone time. Check with your time of observation above. (For a precise method, see Exercise 13, Conversion of Sidereal Time to Mean Solar Time, using *The American Ephemeris and Nautical Almanac.*)

5 determination of right ascension and declination

You can obtain approximate right ascensions and declinations of visible objects by using your starfinder. Align the instrument and set the L.S.T. Then for any object that can be seen in the viewing tube, you can read off the right ascension and declination on the appropriate scales. Indeed, you can identify a fairly bright star in this way. In the list of brightest stars, the stars are listed in increasing order of right ascension. Match with appropriate declination and magnitude, and your identification is complete;

activity

Find the right ascension and the declination for each of two stars. Identify them and compare your values with the values given in the *Observer's Handbook* or some other source.

Star 1.

R.A. _____ (starfinder)

Dec. _____ (starfinder)

Name of star _____

R.A. _____ (book value)

Dec. _____ (book value)

Star 2.

R.A. _____ (starfinder)

Dec. _____ (starfinder)

Name of star _____

R.A. _____ (book value)

Dec. _____ (book value)

6   determination of latitude and longitude (special project)

The experiment described in the following pages makes use of a starfinder designed for use in latitude 40° N. Study the example carefully so that you see clearly how latitude and longitude are obtained with the given instrument.

activity

Design a similar experiment using a starfinder built for your own latitude. Use a different star to determine, if possible, the latitude and longitude of your own locality. Write a report on your project and present your data in neat form.

Determination of latitude and longitude are best shown by an example. You are somewhere in North America on June 8, 1968, with a starfinder designed for use in latitude 40° N, a copy of the *American Ephemeris and Nautical Almanac* (or equivalent information), and a radio capable of picking up time signals or a watch set accurately to some known Z.T., not necessarily that of the zone you are in. You wish to determine your latitude and longitude approximately.

Assume that you have previously determined a north-south line by the sun-shadow method described in Exercise 11, Shadow Stick Astronomy. Set the Starfinder in the north-south direction. Set L.S.T. = 0^h, R.A. = 0^h. Select a star that you know which is slightly east of the meridian, say α Lib (Zubenelgenubi) whose R.A. = 14^h 49^m 12^s and Dec. = $+15°$ $52'$, but do not make these settings. Suppose a time signal is received indicating that it is 22^h 40^m 00^s Central standard time and that 48^s later you judge that the star is on the meridian, that is, due south. You read the angle $\theta = 26°$ $29'$ on the starfinder when the star is due south.

a. calculation for latitude

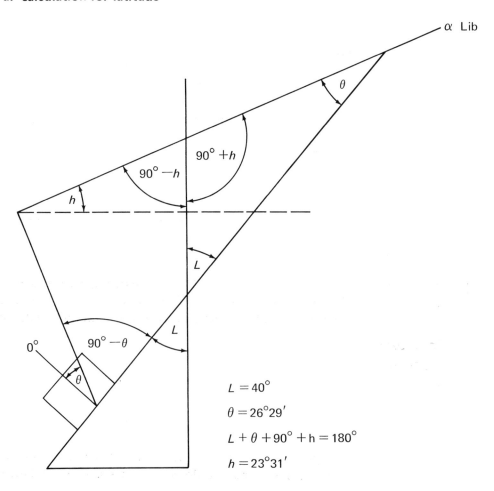

$L = 40°$

$\theta = 26°29'$

$L + \theta + 90° + h = 180°$

$h = 23°31'$

Figure 9-1. Starfinder configuration for the determination of the altitude of α Lib.

coordinates and time

The viewing tube of the starfinder points toward α Lib and the angle θ on the starfinder is shown on the declination scale and is 26° 29′ for this star. (See Figure 9-1). The upper angle on the triangular block is the latitude angle of 40°, since the starfinder was built for this latitude. We first find h, the altitude of α Lib, then determine the latitude by subtracting the sum of the altitude of the star and the declination (ignoring the sign) from 90°. (See Figure 9-2).

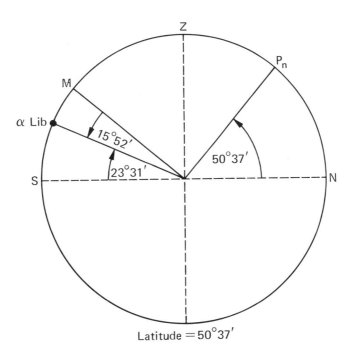

Figure 9-2. The relationship of latitude to the declination and meridian altitude of α Lib.

Note: The latitude of the observer is generally not the same as the latitude for which the starfinder is built.

b. calculation for longitude. When a star is on the meridian,

$$R.A. = L.S.T.$$

From the *American Ephemeris and Nautical Almanac* we determine that the Greenwich sidereal time (G.S.T.) is $17^h\,09^m\,42^s$ corresponding to 0^h Greenwich mean time (G.M.T.), June 9, 1968. Since Central standard time (C.S.T.) was announced, we can calculate the G.M.T. whether or not we are in the Central time zone.

For an observer in west longitude the time at Greenwich is later, and we add

6^h (the zone description) to the C.S.T. of $22^h\ 40^m\ 00^s$. Note that the date has changed, and it is now June 9 at Greenwich. G.S.T. is obtained from the *Ephemeris* or may be calculated from *The Observer's Handbook.* G.M.T. is $4^h\ 40^m\ 00^s$ which is $4^h\ 40^m$ later than the 0^h G.M.T. for which the G.S.T. value of $17^h\ 09^m\ 42^s$ was taken from the *Ephemeris.* In addition, the sidereal clock gains nearly 10^s an hour over the mean solar clock, so the gain of the sidereal clock for $4^h\ 40^m$ is approximately 46^s. This added to the 48^s (48^s from the time of the announced signal till the star reached the meridian) and the $4^h\ 40^m$ gives a total correction of $4^h\ 40^m\ 94^s$.

The new G.S.T. is $21^h\ 51^m\ 16^s$ at the instant the star is due south. The difference between G.S.T. and L.S.T. (same as right ascension in this case since the star was on the meridian) is the longitude of the observer. If G.S.T. is greater than L.S.T., the observer is in west longitude: $7^h\ 02^m\ 04^s$ converted to arc units ($15° = 1^h$, and so on) is $105°\ 31'$ W.

Summarizing the preceding material, we have

Z.T.	$22^h\ 40^m\ 00^s$	June 8, 1968
Z.D.	6^h	
G.M.T.	$4^h\ 40^m\ 00^s$	June 9, 1968
G.S.T.	$17^h\ 09^m\ 42^s$	for 0^h G.M.T. June 9, 1968
Correction for $4^h\ 40^m$ and sidereal clock gain	$4^h\ 40^m\ 94^s$	(includes 48^s)
G.S.T.	$21^h\ 51^m\ 16^s$	for $4^h\ 40^m$ G.M.T. June 9, 1968
R.A. = L.S.T.	$14^h\ 49^m\ 12^s$	
Longitude	$7^h\ 02^m\ 04^s = 105°\ 31'$ W.	

In summary, our latitude is $50°\ 37'$ N. and our longitude is $105°\ 31'$ W. We are at Moose Jaw, Saskatchewan, Canada!

Note: Precise determination of longitude and latitude is somewhat more involved than the procedure described suggests. The use of the starfinder, which is a relatively crude instrument, does not justify the high degree of precision indicated in these calculations.

exercise

10

locating celestial objects with a coordinate grid

1 materials

Coordinate grid, pin, see Appendix A.

2 purpose

Whatever your latitude and longitude, the coordinate grid (Figure 10–1) will enable you to combine your local sidereal time with the equatorial coordinates of an object to then determine the horizon coordinates of that object. The horizon coordinates, azimuth, and altitude, will enable you to determine whether or not an object is favorably located for viewing or to answer related questions with regard to the sun, stars, planets, comets, and so on.

For definitions, reference may be made to the notes on the Celestial Sphere and Coordinate Systems (Appendix A). For the calculation of sidereal time, Table 6–2 in Exercise 6, Calculation of Sidereal Time, may be used or the method requiring the use of the *American Ephemeris and Nautical Almanac,* as described in this same exercise, may be used. Alternatively, Table 8–1 and the method outlined in Exercise 8, The Starfinder–Part I, will yield the sidereal time within a minute or two.

3 design of the coordinate grid

The underlay and overlay coordinate grid dials, (in Figure 10–5 on transparent acetate sheet on page 293) are alike except for labeling. The extremeties of the parallels are at 15°intervals, and it is seen in Figure 10–2 that the distance between the parallels decreases as the zenith or the celestial pole is approached. In measuring the local hour angle (L.H.A.), Dec., Z_n, and h, foreshortening of the arcs resulting from the need to represent a three-dimensional surface in two dimensions must be compensated for, and readings may often be made to within a few degrees.

Cut out the two circular dials and place the translucent dial containing the point P_n on top of the dial containing the zenith point Z. A pin through the center of the two permits the upper dial to rotate on the lower one.

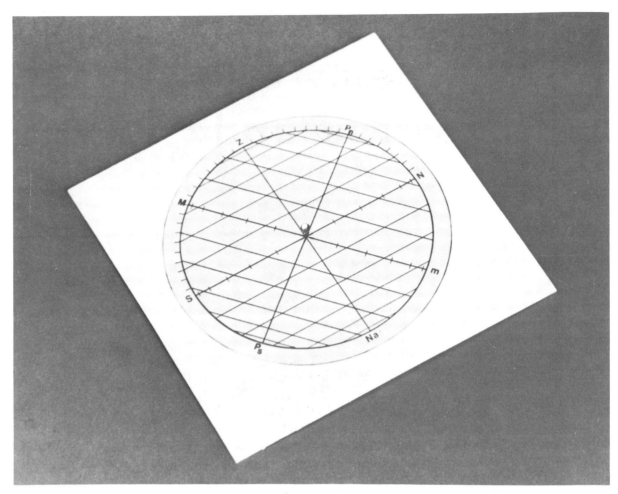

Figure 10-1. Assembled coordinate grid. The dials are fastened to the cardboard by a pin at the center.

4 some things to recall

1. Given the local sidereal time (L.S.T.) and the right ascension (R.A.) of an object, one of the following formulas is applicable for obtaining the local hour angle (L.H.A.) of the object.

$$\text{L.S.T.} - \text{R.A.} = \text{L.H.A.}$$
$$\text{L.S.T.} + 24^h - \text{R.A.} = \text{L.H.A.}$$

2. Local hour angle, measured in hours, minutes, and seconds, is measured from the intersection (at point M) of the upper branch of the observer's meridian with the celestial equator westward along the celestial equator to the foot of the hour circle passing through the object. The hour circle which passes through the body also passes through the celestial poles, P_n and P_s.

coordinates and time

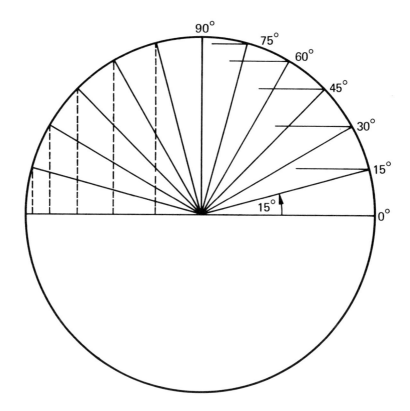

Figure 10-2. System for the design of the coordinate grids. Completed grids are provided in Figure 10-5 on the transparent sheet on page 293.

3. For an observer in north latitude, the elevation of P_n above the north point of the observer's horizon is numerically equal to his latitude. Similarly, for an observer in a southern latitude, the elevation of P_s above the south point of his horizon at S is numerically equal to his latitude.

4. The azimuth of a body is an arc measured from the north point N of the observer's horizon *eastward* along the celestial horizon to the foot of the vertical circle through the body. It is measured in degrees, minutes, and seconds of arc. The vertical circle that passes through the body also passes through the zenith Z and the nadir Na.

5 use of the coordinate grid in determining horizon coordinates

Example 10-1 (See Figure 10-3). An observer is in latitude 40° N and longitude 76° W and observes a star (S_1 on the grid) having R.A. = 14ʰ 40ᵐ Dec. = −10° on May 18 when his Z.T. is 20ʰ 00ᵐ. Describe the position of the star S_1 by estimating its azimuth Z_n and altitude h. (Verify that the position of S_1 on the grid is consistent with the given information.)

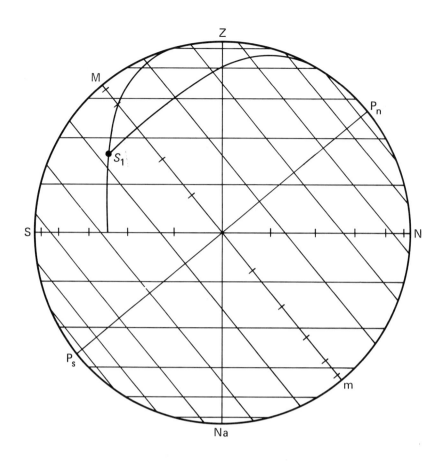

Figure 10-3. Coordinate grid solution for Example 10-1. The star is on the front of the sphere with azimuth 128° and altitude 24°.

Step 1: *Computation of L.S.T.* The student should verify that for the given date, Z.T., and longitude, the observer's L.S.T. is approximately $11^h\,40^m$.

Step 2: *Computation of L.H.A.*

$$\text{L.S.T.} + 24^h - \text{R.A.} = \text{L.H.A.}$$
$$11^h\,40^m + 24^h - 14^h\,40^m = 21^h\,00^m = \text{L.H.A.}$$

We verify that S_1 has been located properly on the equatorial grid by the following two steps:

Step 3: Starting at M measure the L.H.A. $= 21^h\,00^m$ from M (at 0^h) along the Mm line to m (at 12^h) in units of 1^h and return from m along the mM line an additional 9^h for a total of 21^h.

Step 4: We imagine an hour circle (great circle in the equator system) drawn through P_n, S_1, and P_s so that the hour circle passing through the three points intersects the Mm axis at right angles.

We measure 10° south declination by going from this intersection along the hour circle toward P_s. Each parallel division represents 15° as we go along the hour circle.

At this stage we have located the object on the celestial sphere. With the addition of the latitude factor, the horizon coordinates can be found.

We estimate these coordinates by taking the following steps:

Step 5:   Elevate the north celestial pole P_n 40° above the north point of the horizon N. Each division on the lower circle represents 5°. We therefore raise P_n eight divisions above N.

Step 6:   Imagine a vertical circle (great circle in the horizon system) drawn through Z, S_1, and Na so that the vertical circle passing through these three points intersects the S-N axis at right angles. We estimate the altitude to be 24° (the object is above the horizon since it is above the S-N line) by measuring from this intersection along the vertical circle toward Z. Each parallel division represents 15° as we go along the vertical circle.

Step 7:   Azimuth is subject to the following rules:

(a) If the L.H.A. is between 0^h and 12^h, then the azimuth will lie between 180° and 360°.

(b) If the L.H.A. is between 12^h and 24^h, then the azimuth will lie between 0° and 180°.

In our example, the L.H.A. of S_1 is 21^h 00^m. We apply rule (b) and measure from N along the N-S line to where the vertical circle intersects the N-S line. This will between the 8th and 9th division (each division on the N-S line represents 15°), so we estimate the azimuth to be approximately 128°.

For this observer, S_1 has azimuth 128° and altitude 24°. Thus it is 38° south of east and 24° above the horizon.

Star S_1 in the course of a day moves on a line through S_1 and parallel to the line Mm. Where this line intersects the S-N line marks where it will rise and set. For this example the rising azimuth is 105°; the setting azimuth is 255°.

Example 10–2. By using the same right ascension of S_1 but different L.S.T., the L.H.A. of S_1 could be 3^h. The declination remains at $-10°$. Estimate the azimuth Z_n and the altitude h of S_1. Assume that the observer's latitude is 40° N. (See Figure 10–4).

Altitude is the same as before, 24°. Since L.H.A. $= 3^h$ (which is between 0^h and 12^h), the azimuth will be between 180° and 360°. An azimuth of approximately 232° should do nicely. For azimuth we have measured from N along the N-S line to S and back along the S-N line to where the vertical circle through S_1 intersects the S-N line. Thus the object is 52° west of south and 24° above the horizon.

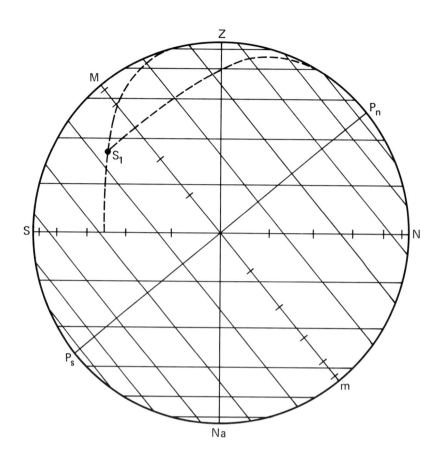

Figure 10-4. Coordinate grid solution for Example 10-2. The star is on the back of the sphere with azimuth 232° and altitude 24°.

coordinate grid problems

1. For an observer in latitude 40° N, the L.H.A. of S_1 is $15^h\,20^m$, Dec. +19°. Verify that the azimuth of S_1 is 50° and that its altitude is −15°. *Note*: The object S_1, subject to the given conditions, would not be visible to the observer because it would lie below the horizon; nevertheless we can describe its position. (At some later time in the day it will be above the horizon.)

2. In Example 10–1, we change the latitude of the observer from 40° N to 55° N; all other data remains the same. Verify that Z_n of S_1 is 132° and that h of S_1 is 13°.

3. In Example 10–1, the observer is in the southern hemisphere at a place where the latitude is 10° S; all other data remains the same. Describe the position of S_1.

ANS. $Z_n = 95°; h = 46°$

4. In Example 10-1, the observer is in latitude 80° N; all other data remains the same. Will he be able to see the object? _____

   Why? _____

   _____

5. An observer is in longitude 80° W, latitude 35° N. He observes the star Sirius (R.A. $6^h 43^m.8$; Dec. $-16° 41'$) on January 6 when the zone time is $20^h 30^m$. Estimate the azimuth and the altitude of this star.

   L.S.T. = _____

   L.H.A. = _____

   Z_n = _____

   h = _____

6. Repeat problem 5 with the observer in latitude 50° N.

   Z_n = _____ h = _____

7. A star has declination +18°. At what latitude will it be circumpolar?

   _____

8. (a) For an observer in latitude 40° N, where does the Sun rise on May 1?

   Z_n = _____ Where does it set? Z_n = _____

   Hint: The declination of the Sun is approximately +15° on May 1.

   (b) What is the maximum altitude of the Sun on this date for the observer? _____

9. For an observer in latitude 55° N, where does the Sun rise on May 1?

   Z_n = _____ Where does it set? Z_n = _____

10. An observer is in latitude 80° N on a day when the Sun's declination is $-15°$. Might he need a flashlight? _____ Why? _____

    _____

11. Assume that the Sun's declination is $+23\frac{1}{2}°$ on June 21. At what latitude will the Sun remain on or above the horizon during the entire day on that date?

12. An observer in latitude 40° N on a very cold day observed that the Sun rose 15° south of east. What was the Sun's declination? _____ Near what date did this probably occur? _____

supplementary problems

1. Show, with the aid of diagrams, that L.S.T. − R.A. = L.H.A. if L.S.T.> R.A. and that L.S.T. + 24^h − R.A. = L.H.A. if L.S.T.< R.A.

2. An observer is in longitude 76° 20′ W, latitude 40° N. On January 15 at Z.T. 20^h he observed a bright star with azimuth 105° and altitude 25°. What was the right ascension and the declination of the star? What star was he observing? R.A. = _____ ; Dec. = _____ ; Star _____

3. An observer in latitude 40° N and longitude 76° 20′ W observed the Pleiades (R.A. 3^h 45^m ; Dec. +24° 02′) at Z.T. 21^h 00^m on February 24 and again the same evening at 23^h 00^m. By approximately how much did the azimuth and the altitude of the Pleiades change in this 2-hour interval?

Z.T. 21^{h}00^m, L.S.T. = _____ , L.H.A. = _____ ,

Z_n = _____ , h = _____ ,

Z.T. 23^h 00^m, L.S.T. = _____ , L.H.A. = _____ ,

Z_n = _____ , h = _____ ,

ΔZ_n = _____ , Δh = _____ .

4. The data in Table 10–1 are for Comet Tago–Sato–Kosaka (1969g) as seen from Lancaster, Pennsylvania, lat. 40° N., long. 5^h 05^m 20^s W.

Table 10-1 Comet 1969g   Z.T. 20^h

Date (1970)	Mag.	R.A.	Dec.	L.S.T.	L.H.A.	Z_n	h
Jan. 20	3.2	0^h 12^m	−20° 53′				
22	3.3	0^h 35^m	−12° 37′				
24	3.6	0^h 55^m	− 4° 36′				
26	3.9	1^h 13^m	+ 2° 45′				
28	4.2	1^h 29^m	+ 9° 13′				
30	4.5	1^h 43^m	+14° 45′				
Feb. 1	4.8	1^h 55^m	+19° 25′				

coordinates and time

4. (a) Complete Table 10–1 for the latitude and longitude of Lancaster, Pennsylvania, or for your own latitude and longitude, whichever your instructor directs.

(b) Would you say that the comet's position, with respect to favorable viewing, is steadily improving? Why? _____

_____

(c) What, if anything, is unfavorable in this situation? _____

_____

_____

shadow stick astronomy

1 materials and references

Shadow stick board (see Figure 11–8 on page 77) millimeter rule, protractor, $\frac{1}{4}$ -in. pointed dowel stick, *Observer's Handbook,* see Appendix A, page 263.

2 purpose

By observing the length and direction of the shadow cast by a vertical stick of known length, we can make some simple and also some rather sophisticated astronomical measurements during the course of a year or part of a year. Your instructor will select those measurements that are appropriate for the time of year and your level of ability. Shadow stick experiments include:

1. Determination of a north-south line or the local meridian.

2. Determination of local apparent noon (noon by the true sun) and altitude of the Sun.

3. Determination of L.M.T. and Z.T.

4. Finding the dates of the solstices.

5. Finding the dates of the equinoxes.

6. Determining latitude.

7. Finding the declination of the Sun.

8. Finding the length of the solar year.

9. Measuring the angle between the planes of the ecliptic and the celestial equator (obliquity).

10. Determining approximate longitude.

11. Determination of the time of day.

Note: In the following exercises it is most important that the shadow stick board be level and that the gnomon be perpendicular to the board.

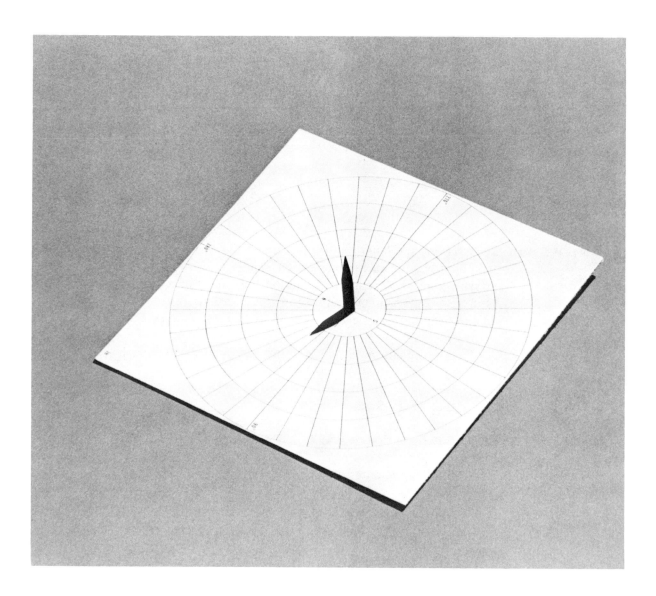

Fig. 11-1. Shadow stick assembly. Note vertical pointed dowel stick used as gnomon. Stick should be about 4-cm in length.

coordinates and time

3 determination of a true north-south line

Place your assembled shadow stick board (see Figure 11-1) in a sunny area and level it. Be sure that the pointed dowel stick, hereafter referred to as the gnomon, is perpendicular to the shadow stick board. An hour or two before noon (no watch is required) the shadow cast by the gnomon will touch one of the concentric circles or some selected point between two concentric circles. Mark this point. Now, sometime past noon the tip of the lengthening shadow will again be on the same circle or at the same distance from the base of the gnomon as before. Mark this point.

Bisect the angle formed by the two shadow points and the base of the gnomon to get the true north-south line. Devise a way to turn the board so that the 90° line on the shadow stick board lies on the north-south direction you have just determined.

You may wish to outline the position of your board in some way after this alignment has been made so that the board may be easily placed in the same position at a future time for other experiments.

4 determination of local apparent noon (noon by the true sun)

The moment when the Sun's shadow is shortest or the shadow falls along the north-south line, is the instant of apparent noon. At apparent noon the Sun's altitude is maximum for that day. Measure the length of the gnomon in millimeters and the length of the shadow in millimeters at the instant that the shadow falls along the north-south line.

activity

1. Record the following:

   Date _____   Length of gnomon _____ mm

   Length of shadow at apparent noon _____ mm

2. Construct a right triangle having length of gnomon as altitude and length of shadow as base. Use a protractor to measure the angle that represents the altitude of the Sun at apparent noon on the date indicated above.

   Record the altitude of the Sun _____ _____ .

3. Repeat the experiment a week or two later if possible and record the following:

Date _____   Length of gnomon _____mm

Length of shadow at apparent noon _____mm

Altitude of Sun _____

4. Account for any difference noted between the lengths of shadows at apparent noon for the two dates.

Note: The altitude of the Sun at any time during the day can be determined by this method of constructing a triangle to scale and using a protractor to measure the altitude of the Sun.

5 determination of local mean time (L.M.T.) and zone time (Z.T.)

At the instant the shadow of the gnomon falls along the north-south line of your properly aligned shadow stick board, it is local apparent noon, and we say that the local apparent time (L.A.T.) is 12^h. The difference between apparent time and mean time is the equation of time (Eq.T.) and the equation L.A.T. − L.M.T. = Eq.T. represents this relation. The equation of time in minutes may be estimated from the graph in Figure 11–2. The equation of time may be positive or negative depending upon the time of year. For a discussion of the apparent Sun and the mean Sun, see Exercise 3, Construction of a Sundial.

activity

Record the following:

Date _____

Longitude _____   Eq.T. (from diagram) _____

L.A.T. (at apparent noon) = $12^h\ 00^m$ L.M.T. = _____

Let $\Delta\lambda$ represent the difference between your longitude and the longitude of the central meridian (some multiple of 15°) of your time zone. Then your

Z.T., or the standard time that you carry on your watch if it is correct, is given by the formula

$$Z.T. - \Delta\lambda = L.M.T.$$ west of the central meridian

or

$$Z.T. + \Delta\lambda = L.M.T.$$ east of the central meridian

Record the following:

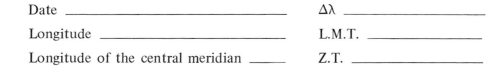

Date _____ $\Delta\lambda$ _____

Longitude _____   L.M.T. _____

Longitude of the central meridian _____   Z.T. _____

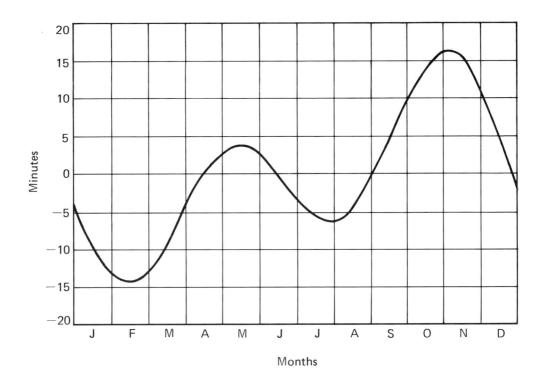

Figure 11-2. Equation of time (local apparent time minus local mean time.)

6 **finding the dates of the summer and winter solstices**   The shortest *noonday* shadow of the year occurs about June 21 when the Sun has maximum altitude for the year. This is the date of the summer solstice. The shadow, at noon, is longest about December 22, the time of the winter solstice.

Write a paragraph or two explaining how you could use the shadow stick board to determine the dates of the solstices.

7 finding the dates of the equinoxes

When the shadows at sunrise and at sunset lie along the east-west line, you have the dates of the equinoxes. The vernal equinox occurs around March 21; the autumnal equinox around September 23. At these times the declination of the Sun is $0°$. Days and nights are of equal length on these dates and the Sun rises due east and sets in the west on these dates regardless of the latitude of the observer.

problems

1. Explain in a paragraph how you could use the shadow stick board to determine the date of an equinox.

2. At the time of the vernal equinox indicate whether the Sun has gone from south declination into north declination or from north declination into south declination. _____

8   **determina-**   At the time of the vernal equinox or the autumnal equinox, which is 6
        tion of   months later, the complement of the Sun's noon altitude is the latitude; that
        latitude   is,

$$90° - \text{altitude of Sun} = \text{latitude of observer}$$

If one knows the declination of the Sun at other times, latitude is determined from the Sun's *noon* altitude by the formula:

$$\text{latitude} = 90° - \text{noon altitude of sun} + \text{declination of sun}$$

or

$$L = 90° - h + \delta \tag{11-1}$$

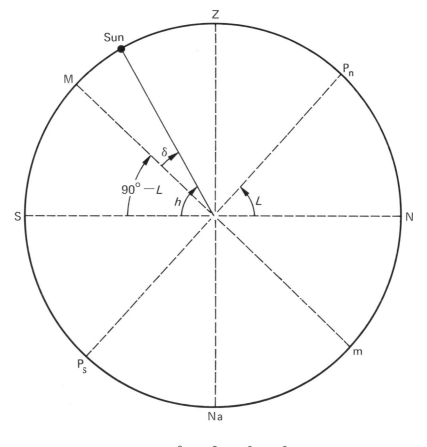

$$L = 90° - 60° + 17° = 47°$$

Figure 11-3. Determination of latitude with Sun in north declination.   See Example 11-1.

Example 11-1 (Figure 11-3). An observer in north latitude recorded the following:

Date: August 5

Dec. of sun: $\delta = +17°$

Noon altitude of sun: $h = 60°$

Example 11-2 (Figure 11-4). An observer in north latitude recorded the following:

Date: January 25

Dec. of sun: $\delta = -19°$

Noon altitude of sun: $h = 42°$

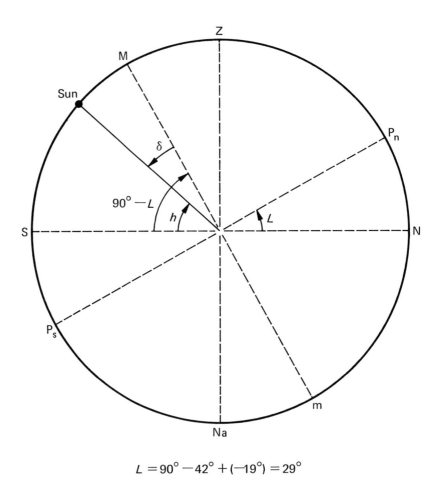

$$L = 90° - 42° + (-19°) = 29°$$

Figure 11-4. Determination of latitude with Sun in south declination. See Example 11-2.

1. Use your shadow stick assembly to determine the meridian altitude of the Sun at apparent noon as described in Section 4 of this exercise. Record the following:

   Date: _____

   Dec. of Sun (from *Observer's Handbook*) _____

   Length of gnomon   _____

   Length of shadow   _____

   Altitude of Sun (from triangle)   _____

   Determine your latitude by using formula (11–1), page 67. Latitude _____.

2. (Optional): Describe the procedure you would use to determine your latitude if you were a resident of the southern hemisphere.

9 determining the declination of the sun

At the time of an equinox the declination of the Sun is 0°, and the meridian altitude of the Sun at apparent noon can be determined for that date. The difference between the meridian altitude of the Sun at a later date and the meridian altitude of the Sun at the time of the equinox will yield the declination of the Sun for the later date.

Example 11-3. Latitude 40° N

Date:	March 21 (vernal equinox)
Dec. of Sun:	$\delta = 0°$
Meridian altitude of Sun:	$h_1 = 50°$
Later date:	April 28
Meridian altitude of Sun:	$h_2 = 64°$
Dec. of Sun (April 28):	$h_2 - h_1 = 64° - 50° = +14°$

activity

Use your shadow stick assembly to determine the meridian altitude of the Sun at apparent noon as described in Section 4 of this exercise. Record the following:

Date: _____

Latitude: _____

Length of gnomon: _____

Length of shadow: _____

Altitude of Sun (from triangle): $h_2 =$ _____

Equinox date: _____

Altitude of Sun at equinox (90° − latitude): $h_1 =$ _____

Dec. of Sun (date): $h_2 - h_1 =$ _____

10 finding the length of the solar year

The number of days, say, from summer solstice to the next summer solstice will be the number of days in the solar year. Some other starting point would do as well.

problem

Describe in your own words how you would make observations with a shadow stick board to find the length of the solar year, that is, the tropical year on which our calendar is based.

11 measuring the obliquity

Obliquity is the angle between the planes of the ecliptic and the celestial equator. The numerical value of the maximum declination or the minimum declination is the obliquity and is $23\frac{1}{2}°$ approximately.

problems

1. Using Section 9 of this exercise, explain how you could determine the obliquity.

2. On what date would the declination of the Sun be maximum? _____

3. On what date would the declination of the Sun be minimum? _____

12 approximate longitude

The L.A.T. when the Sun is on the local meridian at apparent noon is 12^h. With the equation of time for the given date we can determine the local mean time (L.M.T.) by use of the formula

$$\text{L.A.T.} - \text{L.M.T.} = \text{Eq.T.}$$

Radio station WWV in Fort Collins, Colorado, braodcasts G.M.T. on frequencies 2.5, 5, 10, and 15 MHz. Station CHU in Ottawa, Canada, transmits on frequencies 3330, 7335, and 14670 kHz and announcements of Eastern Standard Time (E.S.T.) are made in both English and French. (Add 5^h to E.S.T. to get G.M.T.).

With the aid of a radio time signal (or a chronometer set to Greenwich time) we can determine the G.M.T. If the L.M.T. is less than the G.M.T. we are in *west longitude* and G.M.T. $-$ L.M.T. $= \lambda$ where λ is longitude.

If the L.M.T. is greater than the G.M.T. we are in *east longitude* and G.M.T. $-$ L.M.T. $= -\lambda$. Here $-\lambda$ is our longitude *east*.

1. Set a watch to correct G.M.T. Record the following:

   Date: _____

   Equation of time (from graph): _____

   L.A.T. at apparent noon (Sun on meridian): _____ $12^h\ 00^m$ _____

   L.A.T. − Eq.T. = L.M.T. _____

   G.M.T. (when L.A.T. = $12^h\ 00^m$) _____

   G.M.T. − L.M.T. _____ (longitude east or west?)

2. Why is this not an accurate method for determining longitude?

**13 determina-
tion of
time of
day**

To determine the time of day (Z.T.) when the Sun is not at a meridian altitude using a shadow stick is a rather involved problem; it is much easier to to use a sundial specially designed for your latitude. (See Exercise 3, Design of a Horizontal Sundial.) However, it is possible to determine the time of day by use of a shadow stick, and Example 11–4 illustrates the technique.

Example 11-4. On October 20, 1966 a pointed 40.0-mm dowel stick (gnomon) located near an east window cast a shadow approximately 60.6 mm in length (Figure 11–5). For that day the right ascension of the Sun was $13^h\ 38^m$ and the declination of the Sun was $-10°\ 15'$. The observer was in latitude 40° N and longitude 76° 20′ W (Lancaster, Pa.). What was the time of day?

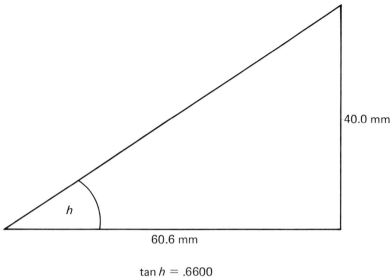

$$\tan h = .6600$$
$$h = 33°26' \text{ (altitude of Sun)}$$

Figure 11-5. Altitude of the Sun. The gnomon was 40.0 mm high and its shadow was 60.6 mm long.

Solution (*Figure 11–6*): In the astronomical triangle P_nBZ the co-altitude is $90° - 33°\ 26' = 56°\ 34'$ and the arc P_nB is $90° + |\text{dec}| = 100°\ 15'$. The meridian angle t is unknown and the co-latitude is $90° - 40° = 50°$. For this spherical triangle,

$$\cos 56°\ 34' = \cos 100°\ 15' \cos 50° + \sin 100°\ 15' \sin 50° \cos t$$
$$\cos t = .8826$$
$$t = 28°\ 02'$$

$$\text{L.H.A.} = 360° - t = 331°\ 58' = 22^h\ 08^m$$
$$\text{L.S.T.} = \text{L.H.A.} + \text{R.A.} = 22^h\ 08^m + 13^h\ 38^m = 11^h\ 46^m$$

We now convert L.S.T. into L.M.T. and then L.M.T. into Z.T. (See Exercise 13, Conversion of Sidereal Time to Mean Solar Time.)

G.S.T. for 0^h G.M.T.	1^h	52^m	01^s
Table IX correction			50^s
Mean sidereal time for 0^h L.M.T.	1^h	52^m	51^s
Observed L.S.T.	11^h	46^m	00^s
Sidereal interval (difference in reversed order)	9^h	53^m	09^s
Table VIII (subtract)		1^m	37^s
L.M.T.	9^h	51^m	32^s
Longitude difference ($76°\ 20' - 75° = 1°\ 20'$)		5^m	05^s
Z.T.	9^h	56^m	37^s
or approximately	9^h	57^m	

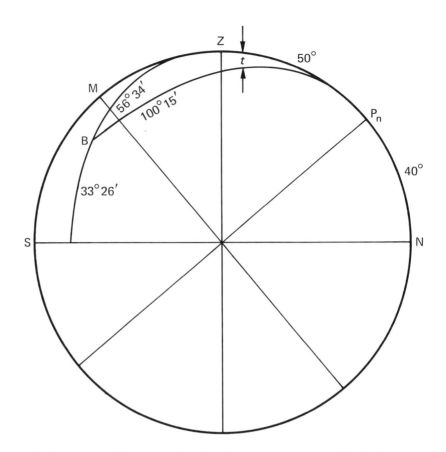

Figure 11-6. The celestial sphere showing the astronomical triangle with vertices at the pole, zenith, and the Sun at B. Solution of the triangle for the meridian angle *t* permits the determination of time.

The recorded correct Z.T. at which the observation was made was 10^h 00^m. Thus it appears that Z.T. can be determined within a few minutes if a pointed dowel stick is carefully placed in a vertical position.

Solution 2 A graphical solution may be obtained by using the coordinate grid of Exercise 10. The intersection of the altitude (33° 26′) and declination (−10° 15′) parallels is shown in Figure 11-7 and a portion of the hour circle through the Sun shows that the L.H.A. of the morning Sun at the time of observation was approximately 22^h 10^m. By substituting the R.A. and the L.H.A. of the Sun into the equation L.S.T. − R.A. = L.H.A., we find the L.S.T. was 11^h 48^m at the time of observation on October 20.

On or about September 21, the L.S.T. and the L.M.T. are numerically equal, and because October 20 was 29 days after September 21, the sidereal clock would have gained, at the rate of 4^m per day, approximately 1^h 56^m in that time interval. Therefore the L.M.T. at the time of observation was 1^h 56^m earlier than the L.S.T. of 11^h 48^m. The L.M.T. of 9^h 52^m for the observer in longitude 76° 20′ W was about 5^m earlier than his Z.T.; therefore his Z.T. was approximately 9^h 57^m.

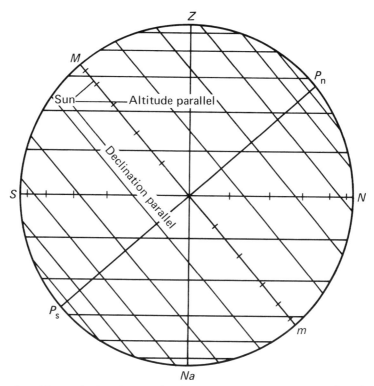

Figure 11-7. Graphical solution for the local hour angle of the morning Sun for use in the determination of time of day.

activity

Try a similar experiment and record the following information:

Latitude _____ Longitude _____

Sun (east/west) of the meridian _____

Correct Z.T. at instant of observation _____

Length of gnomon _____ Length of shadow _____

Date _____ Altitude of Sun _____

R.A. of Sun _____ Dec. of Sun. _____

Meridian angle t _____ (if solution 1 method is used)

    Note: $t = $ L.H.A. if L.H.A. $< 12^h$; $t = 24^h - $ L.H.A. if L.H.A. $> 12^h$

L.H.A. _____ L.S.T. = L.H.A. + R.A. _____

L.M.T. _____ ; $\Delta\lambda$ (difference between longitude and

longitude of central meridan of zone) _____

Z.T. _____ Error in calculated Z.T. _____

shadow stick astronomy

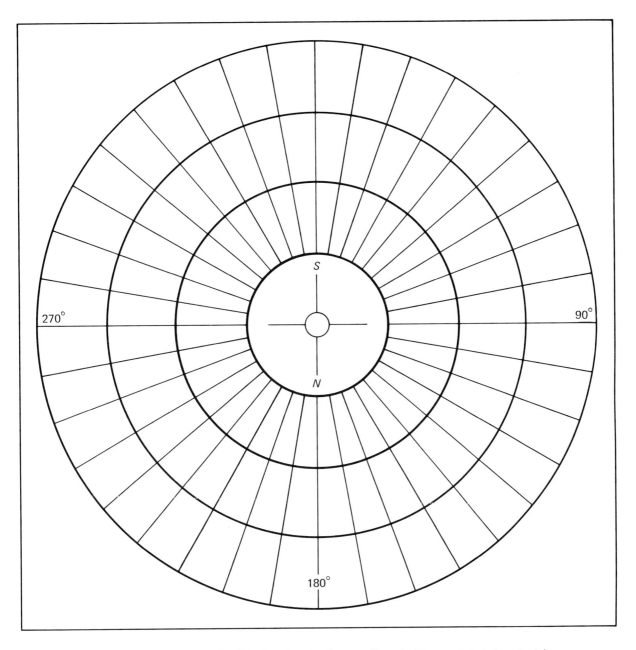

Figure 11-8. Shadow stick dial. Can be glued to cardboard. Place pointed dowel stick vertically at center as shown in Figure 11-1. Length of stick should be about 4 cm.

shadow stick astronomy

77

local mean time and zone time

1 materials and references

None, see Appendix A, page 263.

2 purpose

The measurement of time is based on rotation of the Earth. Mean solar time is uniformly averaged apparent solar time. In this exercise we examine the process of timekeeping and how to determine the local mean time (L.M.T.) and zone time (Z.T.) for an observer in any longitude. Change of date as one crosses the international date line is also considered. Apparent time is considered in Exercise 3, Design of a Horizontal Sundial.

3 conversion of arc into time

The earth rotates through $360°$ in 24 hours, therefore $15° = 60^m$ or $1° = 4^m$. Table 12-1 gives the correspondence between arc units and time units. We need to recall that $1^h = 60^m$, $1^m = 60^s$ for time, and that $1° = 60'$ and $1' = 60''$ for arc.

Table 12-1 Correspondence between arc units and time units

Arc Units	Time Units
$15°$	1^h
$1°$	4^m
$15'$	1^m
$1'$	4^s
$15''$	1^s

problems

1. Convert 84° 47′ 30″ into time. ANS. $5^h 39^m 10^s$

2. Convert 123° 18′ 45″ into time. _____

3. Convert $5^h 05^m 20^s$ into arc. _____

4 local mean time

The Sun's apparent motion along the ecliptic may be thought of as a reflection of the Earth's revolution in its orbit about the Sun. The Sun's motion is nonuniform in that the Earth moves faster in its orbit when it is nearer the Sun (in accordance with Kepler's second law) so that days, based on successive transits of the Sun across a fixed meridian, are not of uniform length.

For timekeeping purposes we invent a fictitious Sun, called the **mean Sun** which moves at a uniform rate eastward along the celestial equator. Basically, the time interval required for the **apparent Sun** (true Sun) to go from the vernal equinox back again to the vernal equinox along the ecliptic is the same as the time required for the mean Sun to go from the vernal equinox back again to the vernal equinox along the celestial equator.

Successive passages of the mean Sun across the meridian fix the length of the mean solar day, which is equal to the average length of an apparent solar day as determined by the apparent Sun. We may define L.M.T. as the local hour angle (L.H.A.) of the mean Sun plus 12^h; that is, L.M.T. = L.H.A. (mean Sun) + 12^h. Mean time varies continuously with the observer's longitude, and the formulas

$$G.M.T. = L.M.T. + \lambda \text{ (west)}$$
$$G.M.T. = L.M.T. - \lambda \text{ (east)}$$

may be used to calculate the L.M.T. if G.M.T. and longitude (λ) are known.

Note: Greenwich mean time, Universal time and Greenwich civil time are synonomous terms.

Example 12-1. What is the L.M.T. and date for an observer in longitude 76° W if the G.M.T. is $23^h 30^m$ on March 4?

Solution

$$\lambda = 76° = 5^h 04^m$$
$$23^h 30^m = L.M.T. + 5^h 04^m$$
$$L.M.T. = 18^h 26^m \text{ March 4}$$

Example 12-2. The L.M.T. for an observer in longitude 80° W is $22^h 30^m$ on March 3. What is the corresponding G.M.T. and date?

Solution

$$\lambda = 80° = 5^h\ 20^m$$
$$\text{G.M.T.} = 22^h\ 30^m + 5^h\ 20^m$$
$$\text{G.M.T.} = 3^h\ 50^m\ \text{March 4} \quad \text{(Note the change in date.)}$$

problems

1. Find the L.M.T. and date for an observer in longitude 124° E if the G.M.T. is $20^h\ 35^m$ on September 30.

   L.M.T. _____   Date _____

2. The L.M.T. for an observer in longitude 123° W is $20^h\ 45^m$ on November 5. What is the G.M.T. and date?

   G.M.T. _____   Date _____

3. The L.M.T. for an observer in longitude 76° 20′ W is $14^h\ 05^m$ on April 27. What is the corresponding L.M.T. and date for an observer in longitude 80° 45′ E? *Hint*: First find the G.M.T. and date.

   G.M.T. _____   Date _____
   L.M.T. _____   Date _____

5 zone time

It was once customary to use only L.M.T., each observer determining his own time by his own observations. With the development of modern communication devices and rapid transit systems this became increasingly inconvenient, and a system of **Standard Time** was introduced.

In its simplest form 24 time zones have been set up and within each zone everybody keeps the same time, called **zone time, Z.T.,** *which is the local mean time* (L.M.T.) *of the standard meridian* for the zone. The standard meridians will be multiples of 15° and each zone, on the average, is 15° wide in longitude, though the boundaries, particularly over land areas, are frequently irregular. The fundamental time is agreed to be G.M.T. People in the first zone east of Greenwich would normally keep time 1^h later than G.M.T. whereas people in the first zone west of Greenwich would keep time 1^h earlier than G.M.T.

In practice the zone boundaries and, indeed, the time kept by a community, state, or nation depends on local preference. The crossing of the international date line (180th meridian) by the mean Sun marks the beginning of a new day for the people in the Greenwich zone (zone 0). Equivalently the crossing of the lower branch of the 75th meridian by the mean Sun marks the beginning of a new day for people in Lancaster, Pa. ($\lambda = 76° \ 20' \ W$) or for anyone who is in zone + 5.

The zone in which an observer finds himself may be described by an integer, called the zone description (Z.D.) The Z.D. generally, is obtained by dividing the observer's longitude by 15 and rounding off the quotient to the nearer integer. The Z.D. will be positive (+) for west longitudes, negative (−) for east longitudes. For example, an observer in longitude 140° W will likely carry zone +9 time; an observer in longitude 50° E will likely carry zone −3 time. Exceptions are numerous, for example, England is in zone 0, but people there carry zone −1 time as do the people in Spain, France, Germany, Norway, and Sweden. There are five standard times in the United States and Canada, namely the Atlantic, Eastern, Central, Mountain, and Pacific. When it is noon at Greenwich, it is 8:00 A.M. Atlantic time, 7:00 A.M. Eastern time, 6:00 A.M. Central time, 5:00 A.M. Mountain time and 4:00 A.M. Pacific time.

G.M.T. and Z.T. for an observer in a given longitude are related by the formula

$$G.M.T. = Z.T. + Z.D.$$

or equivalently $\qquad$ $$Z.T. = G.M.T. - Z.D.$$

where G.M.T. is Greenwich mean time, Z.T. is zone time, and Z.D. is the zone description obtained as described above. If the observer is in west longitude, Greenwich time is later; if the observer is in east longitude, Greenwich time is earlier.

Example 12-3. The Z.T. for an observer in longitude 76° 20' W is $14^h \ 25^m$ on October 21. What is the corresponding Z.T. and date for an observer in longitude 123° 15' E?

Solution 76° 20' W has zone description +5; 123° 15' E has zone description −8

$$Z.T. + Z.D. = G.M.T. = 14^h \ 25^m + 5^h = 19^h \ 25^m \ \text{October 21}$$
$$G.M.T. - Z.D. = Z.T. = 19^h \ 25^m - (-8)^h = 3^h \ 25^m \ \text{October 22}$$

Example 12-4. The Z.T. for an observer in longitude 76° 20' W is $14^h \ 25^m$ on October 21. What is the corresponding L.M.T. and date for an observer in longitude 123° 15' E?

Solution 76° 20' W has zone description +5

$$\lambda = 126° \ 15' = 8^h \ 13^m$$
$$G.M.T. = Z.T. + Z.D. = 14^h \ 25^m + 5^h = 19^h \ 25^m \ \text{October 21}$$

Now $\qquad\qquad$ $$G.M.T. = L.M.T. - \lambda \ (\text{east})$$

and
$$19^h\ 25^m = \text{L.M.T.} - 8^h\ 13^m$$
$$\text{L.M.T.} = 19^h\ 25^m + 8^h\ 13^m$$
$$= 27^h\ 38^m \quad \text{(subtract } 24^h\text{)}$$
$$= 3^h\ 38^m \text{ October 22 (note the change in date)}$$

problems

1. The Z.T. for an observer in longitude 27° E is $22^h\ 25^m$ on December 1. Find the corresponding Z.T., L.M.T., and date for an observer in longitude 77° E.

    Z.T. _____

    L.M.T. _____

    Date _____

2. At Z.T. $23^h\ 00^m$, May 3, a ship is in longitude 179° 30′ W, on a course west. Four hours later the vessel is in longitude 179° 30′ E. Find the Z.T. and date at the latter instant.

    Z.T. _____

    Date _____ ANS. Z.T. 0300, May 5

conversion of sidereal time to mean solar time (z.t.)

1 materials and references

American Ephemeris and Nautical Almanac, 1975, see Appendix A, page 263.

2 purpose

A transit instrument has a small telescope that swings in the plane of the observer's meridian and is used with a sidereal clock and chronograph to determine the sidereal time of passage of a star across the meridian. In this exercise we show how sidereal time may be converted into mean solar time by use of the *Ephemeris.*

3 conversion of sidereal time to zone time

At the instant a star transits the upper branch of the observer's meridian, the right ascension of the star is numerically equal to the local sidereal time (L.S.T.) This is the principle of the meridian transit telescope that may be used for the determination of time. From the L.S.T. thus obtained, zone time (Z.T.) may be determined as follows:

Example 13-1. A transit instrument with sidereal clock and chronograph is located in longitude $5^h 05^m 20.0^s$ W. On December 14, 1975, the star α Ceti at roughly 21^h L.M.T. is due to transit the observer's celestial meridian. The G.M.T. (or Universal time) is roughly 2^h on December 15, and the equation of the equinoxes is approximately 0.8^s (See p. 19 of the 1975 *Ephemeris*). We take the right ascension of α Ceti to be $3^h 01^m 03.1^s$ for December 15, 1975, from the book, *Apparent Places of Fundamental Stars,* 1975. Heidelberg, Astronomisches Rechen-Institut. We wish to determine the Z.T. at the instant of transit.

Page and table references are to the *American Ephemeris and Nautical Almanac, 1975.* G.M.S.T. is Greenwich mean sidereal time and L.M.S.T. is local mean sidereal time.

G.M.S.T. for 0^h G.M.T. Dec. 15	5^h	32^m	06.4^s	p. 19
Reduction for λ (Table IX)			50.2^s	p. 509
Mean sidereal time for 0^h L.M.T.	5^h	32^m	56.6^s	
L.M.S.T. at observation: 3^h 01^m $03.1^s - 0.8^s$	3^h	01^m	02.3^s	
Sidereal interval since 0^h L.M.T.	21^h	28^m	05.7^s	
(subtract in reverse order)				
Reduction to mean solar interval ($-$)		3^m	31.0^s	p. 524
L.M.T.	21^h	24^m	34.7^s	
$\Delta\lambda$ (west)		5^m	20.0^s	
Z.T. Dec. 14, 1975	21^h	29^m	54.7^s	

Check (convert Z.T. to local apparent sidereal time). Find the sidereal time corresponding to zone time 21^h 29^m 54.7^s on December 14, 1975 for the observer in longitude 05^h 05^m 20.0^s W.

G.M.S.T. for 0^h G.M.T. Dec. 15	5^h	32^m	06.4^s	
Reduction for λ (Table IX)			50.2^s	p. 509
L.M.T.	21^h	24^m	34.7^s	
Reduction of L.M.T. to sidereal interval		3^m	31.0^s	p. 511
				Table IX
L.M.S.T.	03^h	01^m	02.3^s	
Equation of equinoxes			0.8^s	
Local apparent sidereal time	03^h	01^m	03.1^s	

problem

An observer is in longitude 7^h 47^m 27.4^s on September 30, 1975 and his observed local apparent sidereal time is 21^h 30^m 20.0^s. Determine the corresponding Z.T.

coordinates and time

unit III

the solar system

Name _____

Section _____ Date _____

telescopic observation of Jupiter

1 materials and refer- ences

Millimeter rule, protractor, *Observer's Handbook, American Ephemeris and Nautical Almanac*, photograph of Jupiter, telescope if available.

2 purpose

This exercise will guide you to some of the interesting features of the planet Jupiter. The planet appears slightly oblate or flattened and, if seeing conditions are good, bands may be seen across the face of the planet. The Great Red Spot may be in position for observation. Some or all of the four Galilean satellites may be seen nearly in line with the planet's equator. Predicted positions of these satellites are given in the *American Ephemeris and Nautical Almanac.*

The orbital motion of Jupiter can be studied because we can calculate its sidereal period from its synodic period of 398.88 days. If we know when Jupiter was last at conjunction or opposition, we can determine its current distance from the Earth and its elongation east or west of the Sun.

3 oblateness of Jupiter

If you look closely at pictures of Jupiter or observe it through a telescope you will notice that it is flattened. The degree of flattening, called oblateness, is calculated by the formula

$$\text{oblateness} = \frac{D_e - D_p}{D_e}$$

where D_e = equatorial diameter and D_p = polar diameter.

1. The equatorial diameter of Jupiter is 143,000 km. Use a millimeter rule to measure the equatorial diameter D_e and the polar diameter D_p from a photograph of Jupiter. Record the following:

$$D_e = \underline{\hspace{4cm}} mm = \underline{\hspace{4cm}} km$$

$$D_p = \underline{\hspace{4cm}} mm = \underline{\hspace{4cm}} km$$

$$\text{oblateness} = \frac{D_e - D_p}{D_e} = \underline{\hspace{4cm}}$$

2. The book value for the oblateness of Jupiter is _____ .

3. How, in general, is the period of rotation of a planet related to its oblateness?

4 observations at the telescope

Jupiter, the largest planet in the solar system, is very bright in the nighttime sky. It's surface is hidden from view by a dense cloud layer covering the planet, which appears as alternating bright and dark bands parallel to Jupiter's equator. These bands result from the rapid rotation of the planet. Jupiter's period of rotation is $9^h 50^m$ at the equator and somewhat longer near the poles.

Jupiter has 13 satellites; the four brightest, Io, Europa, Ganymede, and Callisto are known as the Galilean satellites and were discovered by Galileo in 1610.

	Diameter (km)	*magnitude	Mean Distance from the planet (km)
Io	3250	4.8	421,600
Europa	2880	5.2	671,100
Ganymede	5020	4.5	1,070,200
Callisto	4460	5.5	1,884,500

* At mean opposition distance

We wish to study the surface markings of the planet, the configuration of its principal satellites, and other peculiar characteristics of the planet and its satellites.

Observe the planet with several eyepieces until you find the one that gives the best results under the existing seeing conditions. Use your *Observer's Handbook* and the *American Ephemeris and Nautical Almanac* as necessary in recording your data.

activity

1. Date _____ Longitude _____ Latitude _____

2. At the time of observation record the following:

   Z.T. _____ Estimated magnitude _____

   R.A. of Jupiter _____ Dec. of Jupiter _____

   Estimated Azimuth _____ Estimated altitude _____

3. The constellation in which Jupiter is now located is _____.

4. The brightest star now nearest Jupiter is _____.

5. Carefully sketch the planet showing surface features such as bands, the Great Red Spot (if visible) and the scaled positions of as many of the four Galilean satellites as are visible. Identify each of the four satellites by consulting the ephemeris for Jupiter in the *American Ephemeris and Nautical Almanac.*

5 synodic and sidereal periods of Jupiter

A planet is said to be in conjunction when it is in line with the Sun in the sky and at opposition when it is opposite the Sun in the sky. The synodic period of Jupiter is the interval of time between successive conjunctions or oppositions and been observed to be 398.88 days. A recent conjunction occurred on March 22, 1975, and an opposition occurred on October 13, 1975. Determine from your *Observer's Handbook* when Jupiter last was at conjunction or opposition, or use the information provided to determine the same data.

activity

Record the following:

Last conjunction (date) _____

Last opposition (date) _____

Current date _____

The sidereal period of a planet is the time it takes that planet to orbit the sun once with respect to the stars. The relationship between the synodic period S and the sidereal period P of a superior planet is

$$\frac{1}{S} = \frac{1}{E} - \frac{1}{P}$$

where E, the sidereal period of Earth, is 365.26 days. Solving for P gives 4333.58 days or 11.86 years as the sidereal period of Jupiter.

6 distance and elongation of Jupiter

We can determine the approximate distance from the Earth to Jupiter and the elongation of Jupiter as follows:

1. Plot the positions of Jupiter and Earth at conjunction or opposition, whichever is earlier. This will insure larger angles and greater ease in locating the current positions of Jupiter and Earth (Figure 18–1).

2. Determine the number of days T from the chosen date of last conjunction or opposition to your current date.

3. The sidereal period P of Jupiter is 11.86 years or 4333.58 days, for Earth the sidereal period E is 1 year or 365.26 days.

4. The angular distance Jupiter has moved in its orbit in the time interval T is $360° \times T/P$, whereas Earth in the same time interval T moves through an angular distance $360° \times T/E$ (T, P, and E must be in the same time units).

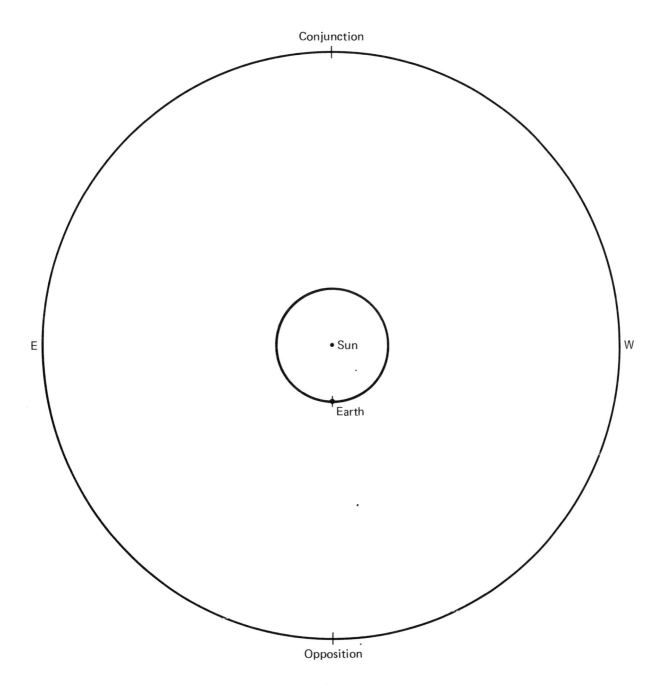

Conjunction

• Sun

Earth

E

W

Opposition

Scale: 15 mm = 1 A.U.

Figure 18-1. Orbits of Earth and Jupiter about the Sun illustrating planetary configurations.

telescopic observation of jupiter

5. Construct these calculated angles to locate the current positions of Jupiter and Earth on Figure 18–1.

6. Draw a line from Earth to the Sun and one from Earth to Jupiter. Measure the distance of Jupiter from Earth and use a protractor to measure the angle directed from the Earth-Sun line to the Earth-Jupiter line. This elongation, east or west, can range from 0° at conjunction to 180° at opposition.

Elongation = _____ (east/west)

Distance = _____mm = _____A.U.

questions

1. How many times more massive is Jupiter than Earth? _____

_____

2. (a) The diameter of Jupiter is _____ .

   (b) The diameter of Earth is _____ .

3. The volume of Jupiter is _____ times that of Earth.

4. Which of Jupiter's satellites is most nearly like our Moon? _____

5. Write a paragraph describing the atmosphere of Jupiter.

supplementary activities

1. Write a report on the Great Red Spot.

2. Describe how the Danish astronomer, Ole Roemer, used the Galilean satellites to provide a fairly accurate measurement of the speed of light.

3. By what factor does Jupiter appear larger in diameter at opposition than at conjunction?

4. Calculate the sidereal period and the mean distance of Jupiter from the Sun given that the synodic period of Jupiter is 398.88 days. Assume that the sidereal period of Earth is 365.26 days.

5. Calculate the approximate difference in stellar magnitudes for Jupiter at opposition and at conjunction. Where is it brightest?

exercise

19

telescopic observation of Saturn

1 materials and references

Millimeter rule, protractor, *Observer's Handbook*, photograph of Saturn, telescope if available.

2 purpose

This exercise will guide you in observing some of the interesting features of the planet Saturn. Saturn is one of the most beautiful sights in the sky because of its rings, and in addition it has a number of satellites that are visible in small telescopes. When the seeing is good, bands may be visible on the disk of the planet.

The motion of Saturn in its orbit can be studied also. The sidereal period of the planet can be calculated from its observed synodic period of 378.09 days, and if we know when Saturn was last at conjunction or opposition, we can find its distance from the Earth and its elongation.

3 the oblateness of Saturn

If you look closely at pictures of Saturn or observe it through a telescope you will notice that the planet itself is slightly flattened. The degree of flattening, called oblateness, is calculated by the formula

$$\text{oblateness} = \frac{D_e - D_p}{D_e}$$

where D_e is the equatorial diameter and D_p is the polar diameter. The equatorial diameter of Saturn is 121,000 km. Use a millimeter rule to measure the equatorial diameter D_e and the polar diameter D_p from a photograph of Saturn.

1. Record the following:

$$D_e = \text{_____} mm = \text{_____} km$$

$$D_p = \text{_____} mm = \text{_____} km$$

$$\text{oblateness} = \text{_____}$$

2. The book value for the oblateness of Saturn is _____ .

3. How in general, is the period of rotation of a planet related to its oblateness?

4 observations at the telescope

Saturn, with its four rings (the fourth was discovered in 1971) is an unique and magnificent sight through a telescope. The rings, paper thin with respect to their diameter, are thought to be from 4 inches to 10 miles in thickness. At times the rings are viewed edge-on to the Earth and are invisible or, at best, appear as a line; when the ring structure is tilted, however, it is extremely bright. Stars can be seen through the rings, so we know that the ring structure is not solid. There is other evidence, too, that shows that the rings are made up of discrete particles.

A moon or satellite must keep a minimum distance, called the **Roche limit**, from its parent body in order to remain intact. The rings of Saturn are within the Roche limit, so either the rings are fragments of a moon that disintegrated when it got too close to Saturn or they are grains of material already near Saturn that could not collect into a single body when the moons of Saturn were first forming.

Observe Saturn with several eyepieces until you find the one that gives the best results under the present seeing conditions. Use your *Observer's Handbook* and textbook as necessary in recording your data.

1. Latitude _____ Longitude _____

   Date _____

2. At the time of observation record the following:

   Zone time _____ Estimated magnitude _____

   R.A. of Saturn _____ Dec. of Saturn _____

   Estimated azimuth _____ Estimated altitude _____

3. The constellation in which Saturn is now located is _____ .

4. The brightest star now nearest Saturn is _____ .

5. Carefully sketch the planet showing surface features such as bands, ring structures, and any satellites that are visible. If seeing is good, you will be able to see the Cassini division, a gap about 4000 kilometers wide between the outer two rings.

5 synodic and sidereal periods of Saturn

A planet is said to be in conjunction when it is in line with Sun in the sky and at opposition when it is opposite the Sun in the sky. The synodic period of Saturn is the interval of time between successive conjunctions or oppositions and has been observed to be 378.09 days. A recent conjunction occurred on July 15, 1975, and an opposition occurred on January 6, 1975. Determine from your *Observer's Handbook* when Saturn was last at conjunction or opposition, or use the information provided to determine the same data.

activity

Record the following:

Last conjunction (date) _____

Last opposition (date) _____

Current date _____

The sidereal period of a planet is the time it takes that planet to orbit the Sun once with respect to the stars. The relationship between the synodic period S and the sidereal period P of a superior planet is

$$\frac{1}{S} = \frac{1}{E} - \frac{1}{P}$$

where E, the sidereal period of Earth, is 365.26 days. Solving for P gives 10759.72 days or 29.46 years as the sidereal period of Saturn.

6 distance and elongation of Saturn

We can determine the approximate distance from the Earth to Saturn and the elongation of Saturn as follows:

1. Plot the positions of Saturn and Earth at conjunction or opposition, whichever is earlier. This will insure larger angles and greater ease in locating the current positions of Saturn and Earth. (Figure 19–1)

2. Determine the number of days T from the chosen date of last conjunction or opposition to your current date.

3. The sidereal period P of Saturn is 29.46 years or 10759.72 days; for Earth the sidereal period E is 1 year or 365.26 days.

4. The angular distance Saturn has moved in its orbit in the time interval T is $360° \times T/P$, whereas Earth in the same time interval T moves through an angular distance $360° \times T/E$ (T, P, and E must be in the same time units.)

5. Construct these calculated angles to locate the current positions of Saturn and Earth on Figure 19–1.

the solar system

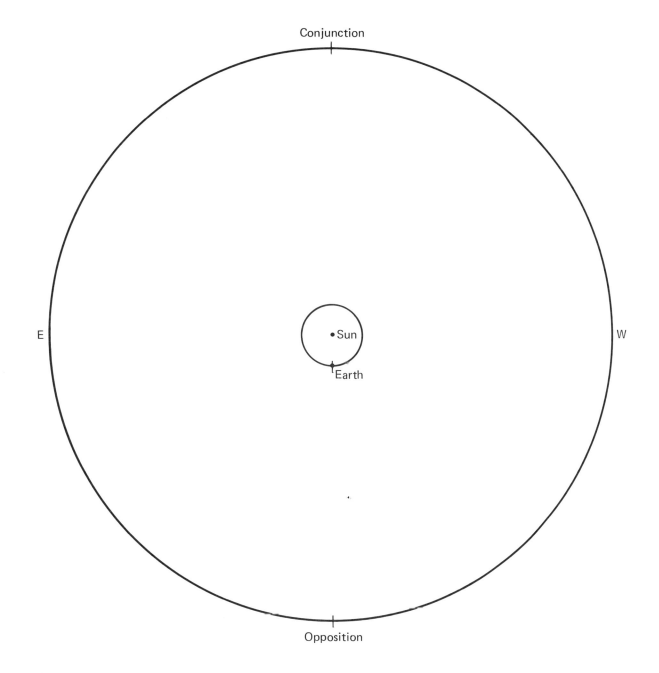

Figure 19-1. Orbits of Earth and Saturn about the Sun illustrating planetary configurations.

6. Draw a line from Earth to the Sun and one from Earth to Saturn. Measure the distance of Saturn from Earth and use a protractor to measure the angle directed from the Earth-Sun line to the Earth-Saturn line. This elongation, east or west, can range from 0° at conjunction to 180° at opposition.

Elongation = _____ (east/west)

Distance = _____ mm = _____ A.U.

questions

1. How many times more massive is Saturn than Earth? _____

2. The diameter of Saturn is _____ .

   The diameter of Earth is _____ .

3. The volume of Saturn is _____ times that of Earth.

4. Write a paragraph or two describing the ring structure of Saturn.

supplementary activities

1. Write a report on the Roche limit.

2. Draw a diagram showing the orientation of the rings of Saturn in its various positions in its orbit as seen by an observer on the Earth.

3. By what factor does Saturn appear larger in diameter at opposition than at conjunction?

4. Calculate the sidereal period and the mean distance of Saturn from the Sun given that the synodic period of Saturn is 378.09 days. Assume that the sidereal period of Earth is 365.26 days.

5. Calculate the approximate difference in stellar magnitudes for Saturn at opposition and at conjunction.

6. Photograph Saturn and report on your exposure times, type of film used, and so on.

lunar features

1 materials   *Sky and Telescope Lunar Map* or other map showing telescopic selenographic latitude and longitude, and telescope for observing the moon.

2 purpose   This exercise will guide you in studying and identifying various lunar features such as mountains and valleys, maria, craters, and so on. The telescope should be used to examine these features preferably at a time near the first quarter-moon.

3 the map   Examine the lunar map and notice that it shows only one side of the Moon. With respect to the stars, the Moon's rotation on its axis is the same as the time it takes to revolve about the Earth, so it always presents the same side to us. Only a score of astronauts have ever seen the back surface of the Moon.

Overlaying the map is a grid of lunar longitude and latitude. In the very center of the map is the position where longitude and latitude are both 0°. To the right and left of 0° longitude lines are drawn from the south pole of the Moon to the north pole at 10° intervals. To the right, longitude lines are marked negative. The lines of latitude are drawn at intervals of 10° also, positive to the north, negative to the south.

Notice that north is at the bottom and south is at the top. Recent Sky and Telescope Lunar Maps show east to the left and west to the right. Older maps have east to the right and west to the left. NASA uses the more recent set of directions. If they had used the old system, the astronauts on the Moon would have found the Sun rising in the west and setting in the east. We will use the more recent directions. In either case the coordinates of the lunar features are the same.

Use your map to complete the following table.

Feature	Latitude	Longitude
_____	+10°	-20°
Bullialdus	_____	_____
Apennine Mts.	_____	_____
_____	+22°	+46°

4 at the tele-scope—seas and high-lands

Indicate the date and the phase of the Moon.

Date _____   Phase _____   Waxing/Waning _____

Study the moon through your telescope and compare it with your map. Most telescopic views of the Moon will look like your map, but a few will be inverted. Your map is drawn to be used with a normal astronomical telescope, which inverts and reverses the image. Study the Moon with your naked eye and try to identify a few major features. You must decide how to hold your map to make it agree with the telescopic image.

Examine the smooth areas of the Moon. These areas are the maria or "seas."

activity

List as many of the maria as you can see at this phase of the Moon.

Early astronomers believed these smooth areas were oceans, but now we know there is no water on the Moon. The men of Apollo 11 visited Mare

Tranquillitatis in July 1969. The coordinates of Tranquillity Base are longitude +24°, latitude +1°. Though it is quite impossible to see anything of the base with any telescope on Earth, locate the position of Tranquillity Base through the telescope. The footprints are still there.

activity

Describe the kind of surface the astronauts found in Mare Tranquillitatis.

The coordinates of the other landing sites are

Apollo Mission	Longitude	Latitude
12	−23°	− 4°
14	−17°	− 3°
15	+ 4°	+25°
16	+16°	−10°
17	+31°	+20°

If possible locate the landing site of Apollo 14, 15, 16, or 17. These sites are located in the lunar highlands, the rough broken high ground on the Moon that covers most of the southern third of the Moon and extends up the center of the visible disk. The maria are evidently the lowlands of the Moon that have been filled by lava and dust. The highlands were chosen despite the danger in making landings in these areas because these highlands, which have not been covered by the maria, represent the exposed original crust of the Moon. Rock samples from these areas were needed to study the origin of the Earth-Moon system.

How old were these samples? _____.

5 **at the tele-scope—craters**

Unless you are observing a full-moon you will be able to see the **terminator**. This is the line that divides sunlight from darkness on the Moon. The terminator is where the sunlight terminates. Notice that near the terminator shadows are long, and it is easy to study the shapes of craters and mountains;

but far from the terminator there are only short shadows, and shapes there are difficult to study. Full-moon is not a good time to study the Moon because, with the sun behind us, there are no shadows at all. Whenever possible choose to study features in the sunlight near the terminator where shadows are long.

activity

Locate one of the following craters and notice the mountain in the center.

	Longitude	Latitude
Petavius	_____	−25°
Delambre	_____	− 2°
Agrippa	+10°	_____
Eratosthenes	−11°	_____
Hansteen	_____	−11°

The origin of these central peaks is not completely understood but may be connected with vulcanism. There is some evidence that volcanoes have been important in the history of the Moon, and a few craters such as Alphonsus have a reputation for fogs and strange glows that suggest the release of gases.

activity

Locate one of the following craters and note the rays of white material that radiate from the crater.

	Longitude	Latitude
Pickering	+48°	_____
Bettinus	_____	−63°
Copernicus	_____	+10°
Reiner	−56°	_____

the solar system

These rays are evidently the remains of material ejected from the crater at the time it was formed by a meteorite. Apparently most craters that we can see are quite old and were formed by giant meteorites. But some may be of volcanic origin, and some are quite recent due to impact of small meteorites.

If possible, locate Plato or one of the other craters listed below.

	Longitude	Latitude
Plato	−10°	+52°
Francastorius	+33°	−21°
Letronne	−42°	−12°

Note that these craters seem to be flooded by the maria material. Thus we can assume that they are older than the maria. But notice that there are craters in the maria material itself, so we must also conclude that crater formation continued after the maria were formed.

Locate the Alpine Valley that runs through the Alps Mountains. This very dramatic feature is very difficult to explain. In good photographs of this region, a rill can be seen running down the center of the valley. Perhaps this is a fault in the lunar crust.

activity

1. Look up rill in your book and write a good definition of it.

2. Locate the straight wall at longitude −8°, latitude −22°. As carefully as you can, sketch the feature and indicate on your sketch which side of the

lunar features

131

wall is highest. The straight wall is evidently an uplift fault. Are there any irregularities along the wall?

additional activities

1. Make a careful sketch about 4 in. across of the moon showing at least 15 features. Include the principal maria, outstanding craters and as many of the following features as you have been able to see on the moon: Piton, Hyginus Cleft, the area north of Capuanus, the Harbinger Mountains, Heraclides Cleft, the Straight Range, Rheita Valley. If Copernicus is visible, chart the rays from it in your sketch.

2. These are all very interesting areas on the moon. If the seeing is good, try to make a very detailed sketch of one or more of these features including all of the detail you can see.

exercise

22

comet magnitudes

1 materials   Logarithm table or calculator.

2 purpose   The magnitude of a comet depends upon its distance from the Sun and its distance from earth as well as other factors relating to its composition. In this exercise we derive a formula for cometary magnitudes and relate it to Comet Tago-Sato-Kosaka (1969g).

3 derivation of formula   Comets, when they are far from the Sun, shine primarily by reflected sunlight, but when they near perihelion or come close to the Sun they also shine by fluorescence. Within 1 A.U. of the Sun the luminance is mostly fluorescence. The combined effect tends to make the comet considerably brighter when it is near the Sun than it would normally be if only the inverse square law of light propagation were involved.

Let d = the distance of the comet from Earth in astronomical units

r = the distance of the comet from the Sun in astronomical units

B = apparent brightness of the comet

L = amount of light leaving the comet

When the comet is at a considerable distance from the Sun,

$$B = \frac{k_1 L}{d^2} \qquad (22\text{-}1)$$

143

where k_1 is a proportionality factor, and

$$L = \frac{k_2}{r^2}$$ (22-2)

where k_2 is a proportionality factor.

Combining the two expressions gives

$$B = \frac{k}{r^2 d^2}$$ (22-3)

where $k = k_1 k_2$.

When the comet is close to the sun, say $r < 1$, the apparent brightness will be considerably greater due to the combined effect mentioned above. Assume B to be of the form

$$B = \frac{k}{r^n d^2}$$ (22-4)

The value of n varies with different comets (from 3 to 6) but is usually near 4. Since $r < 1$ is in the denominator, B increases as r decreases. For the comet near the sun our formula becomes

$$B = \frac{k}{r^4 d^2}$$ (22-5)

Let $B = B_1$ be the apparent brightness of a comet when $d = d_1$ and $r = r_1$; similarly $B = B_2$ when $d = d_2$ and $r = r_2$.

Then

$$B_1 = \frac{k}{r_1^4 d_1^2} \quad \text{and} \quad B_2 = \frac{k}{r_2^4 d_2^2}$$

If $l(m_1)$ and $l(m_2)$ represent the apparent brightnesses of the comet when the apparent magnitudes are m_1 and m_2 respectively, then

$$\frac{B_1}{B_2} = \left(\frac{r_2}{r_1}\right)^4 \left(\frac{d_2}{d_1}\right)^2 = \frac{l(m_1)}{l(m_2)} = (2.512)^{m_2 - m_1}$$ (22-6)

and

$$0.4(m_2 - m_1) = 4 \log\frac{r_2}{r_1} + 2 \log\frac{d_2}{d_1}$$

which simplifies to

$$m_2 - m_1 = 10 \log \frac{r_2}{r_1} + 5 \log \frac{d_2}{d_1} \qquad (22\text{-}7)$$

Suppose $\quad m_1 = m_1^*$ when $r_1 = 1$ A.U. and $d_1 = 1$ A.U.

then $\qquad m_2 = m_1^* + 10 \log r_2 + 5 \log d_2.$ $\qquad (22\text{-}8)$

Example. A partial ephemeris for Comet Tago-Sato-Kosaka (1969g) taken from the IAU Central Bureau for Astronomical Telegrams (#2189) is shown.

Date	R.A.	Dec.	d	r	Magnitude, m
Jan. 16, 1970	$23^h\ 19^m$	$-35°\ 55'$	.409	.772	2.9
18	$23^h\ 46^m$	$-28°\ 49'$	.389	.806	3.0
20	$0^h\ 12^m$	$-20°\ 53'$	.381	.841	3.2
22	$0^h\ 35^m$	$-12°\ 37'$	.384	.877	—
24	$0^h\ 55^m$	$-\ 4°\ 36'$	.397	.912	—

On January 18, 1970, $d_2 = .389$, $r_2 = .806$, $m_2 = 3.0$. Hence,

$$3 = m_1^* + 10 \log .806 + 5 \log .389$$

and $\qquad 3 = m_1^* - .94 - 2.05$

and $\qquad m_1^* = 6.0$

Dropping subscripts and substituting $m_1^* = 6.0$ into equation (22-8) gives

$$m = 6 + 10 \log r + 5 \log d \qquad (22\text{-}9)$$

problems

1. Use equation (22-9) to compute the apparent magnitude of the comet on January 24, 1970.

2. Compare its brightness on January 24 with its brightness on January 18.

3. Plot the positions of the comet on a star chart or celestial globe. Would the comet have been easily visible in the early evening of January 24, 1970, for an observer at your location?

4. If you have constructed the coordinate grid used in Exercise 10, determine the approximate azimuth and altitude of the comet for an observer in latitude 40° N and longitude $5^h \, 05^m$ W for Z.T. 19^h, and for Z.T. 21^h on January 24, 1970.

      Azimuth _____   Altitude _____   Z.T. 19^h

      Azimuth _____   Altitude _____   Z.T. 21^h

unit IV

stars

apparent magnitudes

1 materials and references

Table of logarithms or calculator.

2 purpose

In astronomy the brightness of stars is measured in a system called the magnitude scale. The apparent magnitude of a star refers to the brightness or faintness of the star as we see it from the Earth.

3 apparent magnitude

The scale of magnitudes in use today dates from the Greek astronomer Hipparchus who lived in the third century B.C. In 1856 N. R. Pogson refined the scale by proposing that stars could be called 1st magnitude stars if they were exactly 100 times brighter than 6th magnitude stars. The scale was established such that the pole star had a magnitude of 2.12 and such that two stars whose magnitudes differed by 5 magnitudes were separated in brightness by a factor of exactly 100. The modern magnitude scale is now based on more than one star, but the equivalence between 5 magnitudes and a factor of 100 is still in use.

In addition it was specified that the larger the magnitude number of a star, the fainter the star. This was to make the new system compatible with the classification introduced by Hipparchus.

4 Pogson's law

Pogson proposed that stars be assigned magnitudes by a geometric sequence as follows:

Magnitude number	1	2	3	4	5	6
Apparent brightness	x^5	x^4	x^3	x^2	x^1	1

149

If a 1st magnitude star is 100 times as bright as a 6th magnitude star, then $x^5 = 100$ and x must be 2.512. This constant in the given sequence produces the proper magnitude scale. A 3rd magnitude star is 2.512 times brighter than a 4th magnitude star. A 4th magnitude star is 2.512 times brighter than a 5th magnitude star; thus, the 3rd magnitude star must be 2.512^2 or 6.3 times brighter than the 5th magnitude star.

The decimal division of the magnitude interval was first used by Argelander and Schonfeld. Logically the scale of magnitudes can be continued in both directions without limit. Since there are different ways of observing stars, there are different kinds of magnitudes: visual, photographic, bolometric, and so on. Comparison of two stars must be made within the same system or type of apparent magnitudes.

A study of the preceding discussion will suggest the general formula

$$\frac{L(m)}{L(n)} = (2.512)^{n-m} \tag{23-1}$$

where $L(m)$ and $L(n)$ represent the brightness of stars of magnitudes m and n. An equivalent form of equation (23-1) is

$$\log \frac{L(m)}{L(n)} = 0.4\,(n-m) \tag{23-2}$$

The following two examples illustrate the use of these formulas.

Example 23-1. Procyon has apparent magnitude 0.37, Zubenelgenubi 2.76. Compare their brightnesses.

Solution

$$\frac{L(0.37)}{L(2.76)} = (2.512)^{2.76-0.37} = (2.512)^{2.39}$$
$$= 9.04 \text{ by calculator}$$

If we use logarithm tables, we have

$$\log \frac{L(0.37)}{L(2.76)} = 0.4\,(2.76-0.37) = .956$$

and

$$\frac{L(0.37)}{L(2.76)} = 9.04$$

Procyon is approximately 9 times brighter than Zubenelgenubi.

Example 23-2. Sirius has apparent magnitude -1.42, Procyon 0.37. Compare their brightnesses.

Solution

$$\frac{L(-1.42)}{L(\ 0.37)} = (2.512)^{0.37-(-1.42)} = (2.512)^{1.79}$$

$$= 5.20 \text{ by calculator.}$$

Sirius is approximately 5 times brighter than Procyon.

The scale in Figure 23-1 gives some general information about apparent magnitudes of objects and various telescopes used to study the stars.

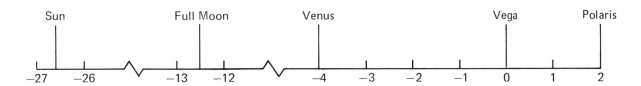

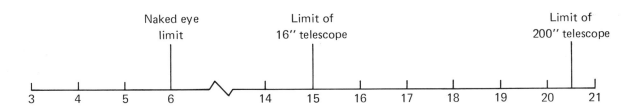

Figure 23-1. Scale of apparent visual magnitudes.

5 limiting magnitude The light gathering power of a telescope depends upon the square of its aperture. We assume that under ideal seeing conditions a 9th magnitude star can be seen visually with a telescope of 1-in. aperture.   Let D be the diameter in inches of a given lens or mirror and $\text{LGP}(D)$ the light gathering power of this D-in. objective. Assume further that $D > 1$ in. Let $L(9)$ be the brightness of a 9th magnitude star and $L(m)$ the brightness of a mth magnitude star. Then

$$\frac{\text{LGP}(D)}{\text{LGP}(\ 1)} = \frac{D^2}{1^2} = \frac{L(9)}{L(m)} = (2.512)^{m-9}$$

Consider $D^2 = (2.512)^{m-9}$. If we take the logarithm of both sides we obtain

$$2 \log D = 0.4(m - 9)$$

which simplifies to

$$m = 9 + 5 \log D$$

For the 100-in. telescope, the limiting visual apparent magnitude is

$$m = 9 + 5 \log 100 = 9 + 5(2) = 19.$$

problems

1. The apparent magnitude of the Sun is −26.7, that of Sirius −1.4. How many stars as bright as Sirius would be required to supply as much light as the Sun?

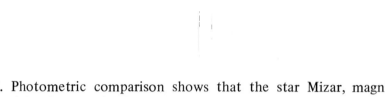

2. Photometric comparison shows that the star Mizar, magnitude 2.4, is 4.37 times as bright as its companion Alcor. What is the magnitude of Alcor?

3. The eclipsing variable Algol declines from a magnitude of 2.2 at maximum to a magnitude of 3.4 at minimum. What is the ratio of brightness at maximum to that at minimum.

4. Suppose a magnitude scale were introduced on which a 5th magnitude star were taken to be 81 times brighter than a 1st magnitude star. How many times brighter would an mth magnitude star be than an nth magnitude star?

5. If star A is barely visible through a 6-in. telescope and star B is just barely visible through a 24-in. telescope, which star is brighter and by what factor? What is the approximate difference in magnitudes of the two stars?

6. What is the limiting visual apparent magnitude of a 24-in. telescope? of a 6-in. telescope?

7. How do photographic time exposures affect the limiting magnitude of a telescope? Explain.

parallax and
absolute magnitude

1 materials

Logarithm table or calculator.

2 purpose

Astronomers measure the distances to the nearer stars by measuring a small angle called the parallax. **Parallax** is expressed in seconds of arc, and the reciprocal of the parallax is the distance to the star in **parsecs**. This exercise will introduce you to parallax, and will demonstrate how the distance and apparent magnitude are related to the absolute magnitude of the star.

**3 trigono-
metric
parallax**

The parallax of a star is the angle p, expressed in seconds of arc, subtended by 1 A.U. at the star's distance, as in Figure 24-1. With the exception of the Sun, parallaxes of all stars are less than 1 second ($1''$) of arc. It is not feasible to draw a diagram to scale because, if p were $1''$ and 1 A.U. were represented by a 1-in. length, the distance in the diagram from the Earth to the star would be 206,265 in. or about $3\frac{1}{4}$ miles.

The skinny triangle in Figure 24–1 for all practical purposes may be replaced by a skinny sector of a circle as in Figure 24–2 in which p is the central angle of the sector and the 1 A.U. distance is the arc of a circle of radius D. For circular sectors we recall that arc divided by radius gives the central angle in radians. To convert degrees to radians we multiply degrees by $\pi/180$. It follows that

$$1'' = \frac{1}{3600}^\circ = \frac{1}{3600} \times \frac{\pi}{180} = \frac{1}{206,265} \text{ radian}$$

Definition: A parsec (pc) is the distance to an object whose parallax is 1″ of arc.

It is a simple matter to show that 1 pc is approximately equal to 206,265 A.U.

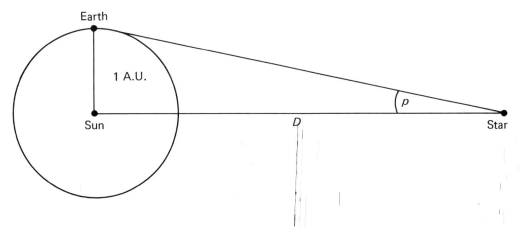

Figure 24-1. A triangle illustrating the relationship between distance and parallax.

In Figure 24–2 if $p = 1''$, then

$$\frac{1\,(\text{A.U.})}{D\,(\text{A.U.})} = \frac{1}{206,265} \text{ radian}$$

and $D = 206,265$ A.U. or 1 pc.

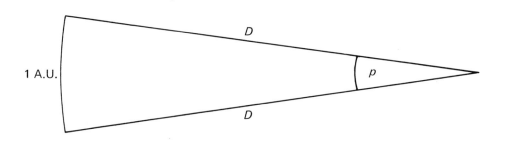

Figure 24-2. A sector that can be used in place of the triangle in Figure 24-1.

problem

If 1 year is 3.156×10^7 seconds, 1 A.U. is 9.3×10^7 miles, and the velocity of light is 186,000 mi/sec, express 1 pc in light years. 1 pc = _____ l.y.

4 parallax and distance

It may be shown that distance varies inversely as parallax, for example, halving the parallax doubles the distance. In Figure 24-3, consider two stars S and S' with parallaxes p and p', respectively. Since arcs x and x' for all practical purposes are equal, let arc $x =$ arc $x' = 1$ A.U. Then

$$\frac{x'}{D'} = \frac{p'}{206,265} \text{ radians}$$

and

$$\frac{x}{D} = \frac{p}{206,265} \text{ radians}$$

Dividing equals by equals and using the relation arc $x =$ arc x' we have

$$\frac{D}{D'} = \frac{p'}{p} \quad \text{or} \quad D = \frac{p'D'}{p}$$

If $p' = 1''$, then $D' = 1$ pc, and it follows that

$$D = \frac{1}{p} \text{ parsecs}$$

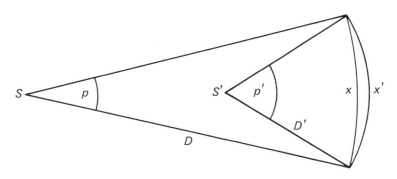

Figure 24-3. Illustration of the inverse relationship between parallax and distance.

Example 24-1. The parallax of a star is $0.05''$. Its distance is $1/.05 = 20$ pc.

problems

1. A star is at a distance of 250 parsecs. Its parallax is _____.

2. A star has parallax $.025''$. Its distance is _____.

3. The nearest star has a parallax of $0.76''$.

    (a) Its distance in parsecs is _____.

    (b) Its distance in light years is _____.

5 absolute magnitude

The absolute magnitude of a star is the apparent magnitude that star would have if it were at a standard distance of 10 parsecs. Recall that the apparent brightness of an object varies inversely as the square of the distance to that object. Hence $L(m) = k/D^2$ where D is the distance in parsecs and $L(m)$ is the brightness of the object having apparent magnitude m. We are assuming that space is transparent.

When the distance D is specified to be 10pc, the apparent magnitude m is equal to the absolute magnitude M. Hence $L(M) = k/10^2$. Dividing equals by equals we get

$$\frac{L(m)}{L(M)} = \frac{10^2}{D^2} = (2.512)^{M-m}.$$

Taking the logarithm of both sides, we have

$$\log 10^2 - \log D^2 = \log (2.512)^{M-m}$$

or

$$2 - 2 \log D = 0.4 \, (M - m)$$

and finally

$$M = m + 5 - 5 \log D$$

If we know any two quantities in the above equation, we can solve for the third quantity. Generally m is known and if the distance D of a star is known, we can find the absolute magnitude M of the star. If we wish to find D, then m and M must be available. In some cases M may be determined by use of the Hertzsprung-Russell diagram, as we shall see in a later exercise.

Example 24-2. Find the absolute magnitude of the Sun given that the Sun is at a distance of 1 A.U. = 1/206,265 pc and the apparent magnitude of the Sun is −26.7. Substituting these values into the formula, we have

$$M = -26.7 + 5 - 5 \log 1/206,265$$
$$= -26.7 + 5 - 5(\log 1 - \log 206,265)$$
$$= -26.7 + 5 + 5 \log 206,265$$
$$= 4.9$$

This is the apparent magnitude the Sun would have if it were at a distance of 10 pc from us.

problems

1. If the Milky Way contains 100 billion stars (10^{11} stars) each as luminous as the sun, what would be the absolute magnitude M of the Milky Way?

2. If $m = 13.5$ and $M = 10$, find the distance D.

3. What would be the apparent magnitude of Rigel if it were at a distance of 1 A.U.? Assume that M for Rigel is -7.1.

4. Is it likely that a planet could exist at the distance of 1 A.U. from Rigel? _____ _____

5. What relationship would exist between the apparent and absolute magnitudes if the standard distance were 30pc instead of 10pc?

6. The luminosity of a star is its total brightness compared with that of the Sun at the same distance, 10pc. If we take the absolute magnitude of the Sun to be 4.9 and the luminosity of the Sun as 1, then an absolute magnitude of 2.4 for Altair implies that the luminosity of Altair is 10.0. If the absolute magnitude of Sirius is 1.3, what is its luminosity?

the grating spectroscope

1 materials Scissors, paper punch, paper clip, rubber cement, razor blade, straight edge, transmission grating replica (Edmund Scientific Co.), Geisler tubes of hydrogen, helium, and so on, if available.

2 purpose This exercise will introduce you to the wave nature of light and the phenomenon called interference. You will build your own spectroscope and use it to examine the spectra of some common light sources. If they are available, some Geisler tubes will be set up for you to study.

3 the grating The grating you have is very delicate. Do not touch the grating material itself as fingerprints will damage it. Do not look at the sun with the grating.

The grating plastic contains 13,400 small grooves per inch. These grooves produce the phenomenon called interference in the light passing through it. The result is a spectrum produced by breaking up the light into its various colors. Hold the grating by its cardboard frame near your eye and look at a window or light. Turn the grating until you can see the color fringes easily.

4 interference Notice that the indigo fringe is closest to the light source and that the red fringe is furthest away. When you look in the direction of the red fringe you see light scattered by a number of the grooves in the grating. Each groove is at a slightly different distance from your eye, as shown in Figure 25–1. Light striking one groove and reaching your eye does not have to travel as far as light striking the next groove and reaching your eye. The result is that the

161

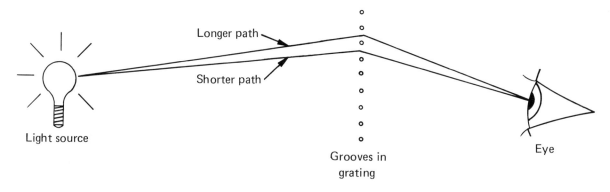

Figure 25-1. Light scattered from different grooves in the diffraction grating travel different path lengths.

light from these two grooves does not arrive at your eye at the same time but, rather, the light from the nearer groove arrives a split second earlier than the light from the farther groove. If light were tiny particles, this delay would make no difference and we would see both "particles" of light with no trouble. However, light is not a particle; it is something that sometimes behaves as a wave and sometimes as a particle. In this case the wave nature of light produces interference.

If the two waves leave the light source together, then their peaks and their valleys will be lined up. But, as we have seen, when they strike the grooves and then reach our eye, one travels a shorter path and arrives earlier. If the two waves arrive so that the peak of one coincides with the valley of the other, they will cancel each other out and there will be no light at all! This is called **destructive interference** and is shown in Figure 25-2. If the waves arrive so that the peak of one coincides with any peak of the other they will add together and we will be able to see them. This is called **constructive interference.**

Whether the interference is constructive or destructive depends not only on the amount of delay but also on the wavelength of the light waves involved. When we look at the red fringe we are looking at a part of the grating where waves of blue, green, and yellow light interfere with themselves destructively but where red light, because of its longer wavelength, interferes with itself constructively. So we see red. If the light source gave off no red waves to start with, we would of course see nothing at all in the red direction.

activity

Look through the grating again and notice that the red fringe is farther from the light source than the blue fringe. This is because red light has a longer wavelength than blue light. List the colors you can see in order of increasing wavelength.

Short wavelengths   Long wavelengths

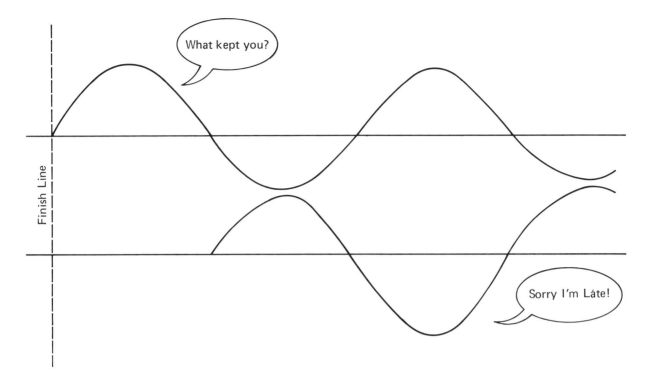

Figure 25-2. Destructive interference. When the peaks of one wave coincide with the valleys of another wave, cancellation occurs.

5 wavelength and color

Our eyes can tell one color from another because each color has its own wavelength range. The deep indigo color, for example, has a wavelength range from 0.000041 to 0.000046 cm (centimeters), whereas blue light has a range from 0.000046 to 0.000051 cm, and so on. Of course the transition from one color to another is gradual so exact wavelengths are not given. When scientists first began to understand optical interference, they realized that light could be a wave and that the wavelengths were very short. In fact, the wavelengths were so short that it was inconvenient to measure them in centimeters, so a new unit of length was proposed, the angstrom (Å). This new unit of length is only one ten billionth of a meter (one hundred millionth of a centimeter), and in angstroms the wavelength of indigo light ranges from 4100 to 4600 Å.

problems

1. Approximately what would the wavelength range of blue light be in angstroms? _____ Å

the grating spectroscope

163

2. The central wavelength of yellow light is about 5800 Å. How long is that

in centimeters? _____ .

3. In your grating there are 13,400 grooves/in. or about 5,300 grooves/cm. This means that the distance between two grooves is about 1/5300 cm.

How far apart are the grooves in angstroms? _____Å

4. If the wavelength of red light is approximately 6200 Å, how many waves of red light would fit between two adjacent grooves? _____

6 the spectro-scope

Cut out the corners of the stiff paper figure (Figure 25–4a and 4b) provided on pages 283 and 285. Leave the tabs so the spectroscope can be assembled into a box. Use a paper punch to punch a hole in the indicated location. It may be necessary to cut out the small wedge in order to make your paper punch reach the hole.

Use the razor blade to cut the slit opposite the hole. This slit admits the light to the spectroscope, so if the slit is too narrow the spectrum will be very faint, but if the slit is too wide the spectrum will be blurred and indistinct. A width of 1/16- to 1/32-in. is best.

Use a straight edge and hard pencil or nail to scribe the box on the fold lines and then fold the box and use rubber cement to glue the box together. Put the grating inside the box at the hole and cement it or secure it with the paper clip.

Look through the hole while pointing the spectroscope at a bright light (not the sun). You should see a spectrum above the scale. If not, remove the grating, rotate it one quarter turn and replace it.

7 the con-tinuous spectrum

Use the spectroscope to look at an incandescent light. In an incandescent light electricity flowing through the filament heats it to a temperature of about 5000 to 6000°K. At this temperature the filament glows, giving off light of all different colors. Our eye sees this light as white, but through the spectroscope our eye can see these colors separately.

Notice that the colors are all present and there are no special bright areas and no dark areas. The spectrum is smooth and continuous. This kind of spectrum is called a continuous spectrum.

Table 25-1 Wavelengths of the Colors

Color	Approximate Wavelength (Å)
Indigo	4300
Blue	4800
Green	5400
Yellow	5800
Red	6500
Deep red	7000

8 emission spectra

Use your grating to study some fluorescent lights. It is possible to see not only a continuous spectrum but also bright indigo, green, and yellow lines in the spectrum. You will find that the yellow line is actually two lines very close together.

Table 25-2 Emission Lines of Mercury

Line	Wavelength (Å)
Indigo	4358
Green	5460
Yellow	5769
Yellow	5790

These lines are produced by vaporized mercury inside the tube of the fluorescent lamp. These lines and some others that are too faint for us to see are a "fingerprint" of mercury. Whenever we see this set of lines we know that mercury is present. If you have the opportunity, use your grating to study the light from mercury vapor street lights, iodine vapor street lights, and the light from "neon" signs. You will find different "fingerprints" because many different gasses are used in these different lamps. Different gasses give off different wavelengths of light and produce different colors. Mercury vapor lamps are bluish because there is no bright line in the red part of the mercury spectrum. The iodine lamps are pink, however, because iodine does produce some red lines in its spectrum.

These bright lines in the spectra are called **emission lines**, and spectra that show emission lines are called **emission spectra**. When an astronomer sees an emission spectrum he knows he is looking at low pressure excited gas like the low pressure gas found inside fluorescent lights.

9 spectral identifications

Your instructor will set up some Geisler tubes, which work much like "neon" signs. A high voltage is applied to the tubes and the resulting flow of current through the gas excites the gas atoms to higher energy levels. When the gas

the grating spectroscope

atoms return to their natural energy levels, they give up the extra energy in the form of photons of light. Compare the mercury tube spectrum with the mercury spectrum visible in fluorescent lights.

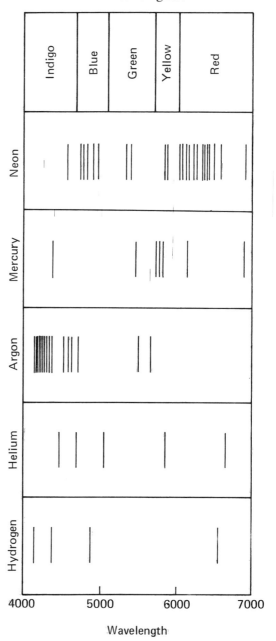

Figure 25-3. Spectral line patterns for several elements.

In Figure 25-3 the spectra of five elements have been sketched. Each black line in the drawing represents a bright line in the spectrum. Red is to the right and indigo is to the left. Compare the mercury tube spectrum with the sketch for mercury. Cross out any lines you cannot see. There is some variation in the ability of different people to see the red and deep indigo lines.

activity

Your instructor will set up three tubes. Study their spectra and use the drawing to identify the elements. Each tube contains only one element.

Tube 1 _____   Tube 2 _____   Tube 3 _____

If you have an opportunity, use your grating to study the spectra of some "neon" signs and see if you can identify the elements in them. This is much the same process an astronomer goes through when he studies a star to discover its composition.

10 the solar spectrum

Whenever you observe the Sun, beware! It is very bright and can permanently damage your eyes. It is possible, however, to view the solar spectrum safely with the spectroscope, but you must not view the Sun directly.

Use the spectroscope to observe light reflected from a white sheet of paper, a white cloud, or a white wall in direct sunlight.

If the slit in your spectroscope is narrow enough you will be able to see not only a continuous spectrum but a number of faint dark lines. The continuous spectrum is emitted by the hot surface of the Sun called the photosphere. As that light travels outward through the gaseous atmosphere of the Sun, various elements in the atmosphere absorb those photons that have just the right energy to raise the electrons to higher energy levels. In the Geisler tubes photons of specific wavelengths were given off when electrons moved to lower energy levels, and we saw emission spectra. In this case, photons are absorbed, thus moving the electrons upward in energy, and we see an **absorption spectrum**. The wavelengths of the lines will be the same for the same kinds of atoms. The only thing that has changed is that photons are absorbed instead of being emitted.

If you study the spectrum you will be able to see faint dark lines in the blue-green, in the green, and in the yellow. The blue-green line is the blue-green line of hydrogen. The line is called the H beta Balmer line. The green line is actually three lines caused by vaporized magnesium. The yellow line is two lines known as sodium D lines. Try to estimate the wavelengths of these lines from your spectroscope and compare them with those given in Table 25–3.

Table 25–3 Strong Lines in the Solar Spectrum

Wavelength (Å)	Fraunhofer Letter	Line
7594	A	Oxygen in our atmosphere
6867	B	Oxygen in our atmosphere
6563	C	Hydrogen alpha
5896	D_1	Sodium
5890	D_2	Sodium
5270	E_1	Iron
5183–5168	E_2	Magnesium (3 lines)
4861	F	Hydrogen beta
4308	G	G band of many lines
3968	H	Calcium
3933	K	Calcium

Which of the lines listed in Table 25–3 can you see? What you can see depends on the width of the slit, the brightness of the light, and how sensitive your eyes are. It may help to make a lid for your spectroscope and to line it with black paper.

The calcium H and K lines are very important in astronomy, and they are very strong in the Sun's spectrum; however, they are so far into the violet that few if any people can see them. Examine the spectrum you can see and cross off the spectral lines in Table 25–3 that are too far into the red or violet for you to see.

Compare the spectrum you see with the solar spectrum printed in your text book. Can you locate any of the lines above in the solar spectrum?

exercise

26

black body radiation

1 materials   Millimeter rule.

2 purpose   This exercise will introduce you to black body radiation. This is important to astronomers because nearly all stars radiate energy as fair approximations of black bodies. This exercise will show that hot stars radiate more of their energy at shorter wavelengths than cooler stars. We also compare the total energy radiated by black bodies of different temperatures and use this knowledge to determine the radii of stars.

**3 black body
  radiation**   We may think of a black body as a hypothetical perfect absorber and radiator which absorbs all radiant energy incident upon it, and reradiates the energy in accordance with the temperature of the black body. Max Planck, around 1900, determined how the radiated energy is related to temperature and wavelength. The Planck equation gives the amount of energy E radiated at a wavelength λ by a black body of temperature T. This equation is

$$E(\lambda, T) = \frac{2\pi hc^2}{\lambda^5} \frac{1}{e^{hc/\lambda kT} - 1} \text{ ergs cm}^{-2} \text{ sec}^{-1} \text{ cm}^{-1}$$

where h is Planck's constant, k is the Boltzmann constant, c is the speed of light, and e is 2.718 .... Although we will not use this equation for any calculations in this exercise, notice that it specifies that a black body with a temperature other than zero must radiate some energy at every wavelength.

  If the temperature of a black body is given, we could use the Planck equation to calculate E, the amount of energy radiated by $1\,cm^2$ of its surface in 1 sec at any given wavelength. A plot of E versus λ results in a black body curve such as the one shown in Figure 26–1. This curve has been plotted for $T = 5000°K$. Table 26–1 contains the data used to plot this curve plus data for two other black bodies with temperatures of $5500°K$ and $6000°K$. Plot the two remaining curves and sketch in smooth curves to connect the plotted points. The wavelengths are given in angstrom units and one unit of E in the table and figure represents 10^{14} ergs cm^{-2} sec^{-1} of energy for each centimeter of wavelength interval.

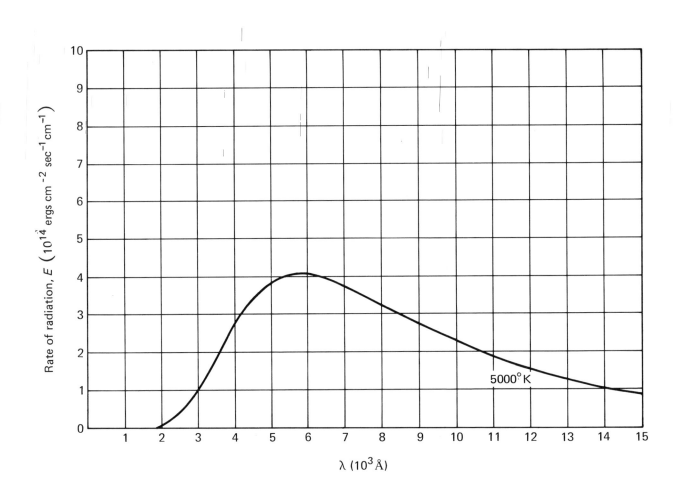

Figure 26-1. Graph for plotting black body curves from Table 26-1. Curve for a black body of $5000°$ K is shown.

Table 26-1 E (λ, T) for Black Body Radiation

λ(Å)	5000°K	5500°K	6000°K	λ(Å)	5000°K	5500°K	6000°K
0	0	0	0	8,000	3.2	4.5	6.0
1,000	0.0	0.0	0.0	9,000	2.7	3.6	4.7
2,000	0.1	0.2	0.7	10,000	2.2	2.9	3.7
3,000	1.0	2.5	5.2	11,000	1.8	2.4	3.0
4,000	2.7	5.3	9.0	12,000	1.5	1.9	2.4
5,000	3.8	6.4	9.9	13,000	1.2	1.6	1.9
6,000	4.0	6.2	9.0	14,000	1.0	1.3	1.5
7,000	3.7	5.4	7.4	15,000	0.8	1.0	1.2

Notice that at a wavelength of 1000 Å the amount of energy radiated by these objects is so small that we cannot graph it, and we record it as 0.0 in the table. We know, however, that these objects must radiate some energy at this wavelength. Only at the nonsense wavelength of zero do objects radiate no energy at all.

4 Wien's law Wien's law states that the wavelength at which the maximum amount of energy is emitted by a black body varies inversely as the temperature. If we let λ_{max} denote the wavelength at which the maximum amount of energy is emitted, then Wien's formula is

$$\lambda_{max} = \frac{0.2897}{T} \times 10^8 \text{Å}.$$

problem

For each curve in Figure 26-1, estimate from the curve the wavelength of maximum energy emission, and then calculate λ_{max} from the Wien equation

Estimated

$\lambda_{max}(5000°\text{K}) = $ _____ Å

$\lambda_{max}(5500°\text{K}) = $ _____ Å

$\lambda_{max}(6000°\text{K}) = $ _____ Å

Calculated

$\lambda_{max}(5000°\text{K}) = $ _____ Å

$\lambda_{max}(5500°\text{K}) = $ _____ Å

$\lambda_{max}(6000°\text{K}) = $ _____ Å

Notice that as T increases, λ_{max} decreases.

black body radiation   **171**

5 Stefan-Boltzmann law

The Stefan-Boltzmann law says that the total amount of energy radiated by a black body at all wavelengths by $1\,cm^2$ of surface in $1\,sec$ is proportional to the fourth power of the temperature. The formula is

$$E(T) = \sigma T^4 \text{ ergs cm}^{-2} \text{ sec}^{-1}$$

where σ is 5.672×10^{-5} ergs cm^{-2} deg^{-4} sec^{-1} and T is temperature in Kelvin degrees. The total amount of energy radiated is proportional to the area under the black body curve. The more area under the curve, the more energy the body radiates.

There are several ways to compare the total amount of radiation emitted by two black bodies at different temperatures. One approximation is obtained by counting the number of squares under each of the two curves and then taking the ratio.

problems

Suppose star A has surface temperature $6000°K$ and star B of the same size has surface temperature $5000°K$. Compare the total energy emitted by star A with that of star B by counting squares under the appropriate curves in Figure 26–1. Estimate areas to the nearest tenth of a square unit.

1. (a) Approximate number of squares under the $6000°K$ curve is_____.

   (b) Approximate number of squares under the $5000°K$ curve is_____.

   (c) How many times more luminous is star A than star B?_____

2. (a) Use the Stefan-Boltzmann equation to compute the ratio of total energies emitted by the two stars.

$$\frac{E(6000°)}{E(5000°)} = \underline{\hspace{3cm}}$$

   (b) Calculate, using the Stefan-Boltzmann equation, the factor by which the radiation increases if the temperature of a black body is tripled.

$$\frac{E(3T)}{E(T)} = \underline{\hspace{3cm}}$$

6 interpretation of the black body radiation curves

Examination of the three curves in Figure 26–1 suggests the following conclusions:

1. The curves do not intersect anywhere. For example, the $T = 5500°K$

172

curve lies entirely above the $T = 5000°K$ curve and likewise the $T = 6000°K$ curve lies entirely above each of the other two curves.

2. For any wavelength λ greater than 0, E is greater than 0.

3. λ_{max} (6000°K) is less than λ_{max} (5500°K) and λ_{max} (5500°K) is less than λ_{max} (5000°K).

We may interpret each of these conclusions in physical terms. For example, the first conclusion (1) may be interpreted to read "A hotter black body or star emits more radiation at all wavelengths than a cooler black body or star."

activity

Express each of the remaining two conclusions in physical terms.

1. Statement 2:

2. Statement 3:

3. Hot stars appear to be blue because they emit most of their energy at short wavelengths (in the blue portion of the spectrum). Cool stars appear to be red because . . .

4. The visible spectrum lies approximately between 4000 and 7500 Å. For the $T = 5000°$ K curve, lightly shade the appropriate area in Figure 26–1 representing the visible portion of the spectrum.

7 computation of stellar radii

The luminosity of a star expressed in ergs per second may be determined by multiplying the surface area of the star in square centimeters by $E = \sigma T^4$ ergs cm^{-2} sec^{-1} (Stefan-Boltzmann equation). For example, suppose we observed

black body radiation

a star at temperature $3000°$K which is 400 times as luminous as the Sun at temperature approximately $6000°$K. (The factor 400 may be determined by comparing the absolute magnitudes of the two stars). The area of a sphere of radius R is given by $4\pi R^2$.

Temperature of Sun: $T_\odot = 6000°$
Temperature of star: $T_\star = 3000°$
Luminosity of Sun: $L_\odot$
Luminosity of star: $L_\star = 400L_\odot$
Radius of star: $R_\star$
Radius of Sun: $R_\odot$

From
$$\frac{L_\star}{L_\odot} = 400 = \frac{4\pi R_\star^2 (3000)^4}{4\pi R_\odot^2 (6000)^4}$$

we obtain
$$\left(\frac{R_\star}{R_\odot}\right)^2 = 6400$$

and
$$R_\star = 80 R_\odot$$

This star, cooler than the Sun but 400 times as luminous as the Sun, is a giant star with radius 80 times the radius of the Sun. The surface area of this star is 6400 times the surface area of the Sun.

problem

The absolute magnitude of the Sun is approximately 4.9, that of another star approximately 7.9. It can be shown that the Sun is therefore approximately 16 times as luminous as the star. If the temperature of the Sun is $6000°$K, and the temperature of the star is $9000°$K, compare the surface areas of the Sun and the star.

$$\frac{\text{Area of Sun}}{\text{Area of star}} = \underline{\hspace{4cm}}$$

exercise

27

the flow of energy out of the sun

1 material

One die.

2 purpose

This exercise demonstrates how energy in the form of radiation flows out of the Sun. This flow is not smooth and uniform because each photon of radiation can interact with the atoms it encounters and its path can be affected in some random manner. The photon's path becomes a very crooked line, a three-dimensional random walk, as the radiation is repeatedly absorbed, reradiated, and scattered on its way from the center to the surface where it escapes into space.

3 absorption and scattering

Inside the Sun most atoms are ionized, but if a photon does encounter an atom that has an electron in an orbit, the photon may be absorbed and the electron comes free; if this happens we say the atom becomes ionized and the process is called a **bound-free absorption**. Later when the electron recombines with an ion, a photon will be reradiated in some random direction.

If the photon encounters an electron that is already free of the nearby atoms, the photon may be absorbed and the electron's energy increased. This is called a **free-free absorption**. Later the electron may give up some energy in the form of a photon radiated in a new direction.

A third process is not an absorption but is called **electron scattering**. In this case when a photon encounters an electron the electron may oscillate, thereby stealing energy from the photon. The energy is radiated as a new photon in some new direction. Electron scattering works almost as if the photon had bounced off the electron.

In all of these cases, the path of the photon is altered in some random way.

175

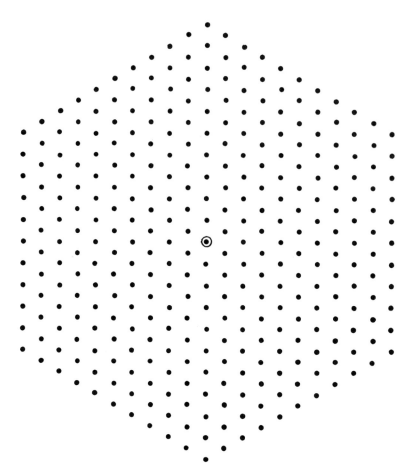

Figure 27-1. Two dimensional representation of a star. Each dot represents an atom or an electron.

4 random walk

Figure 27–1 is a two-dimensional representation of the Sun or a star, where each dot represents an atom or an electron. When a photon encounters a particle, its path may be changed in some random direction. You will use this diagram to move photons from the center (circled dot) to the surface. Each time your photon reaches a particle, roll the die to select randomly the direction of reradiation. The number that comes up on the die multiplied by 2 represents a direction on a clock face. If you roll a 2, the clock face direction is 4 o'clock and you move the photon in the 4 o'clock direction to the next particle. Mark the path of your photon in pencil, and count the number of interactions (rolls) required for the photon to leave the surface of the star. As you do this, keep in mind the various processes that can affect the path of a photon in a star.

Record the number of rolls you needed to have your photon escape from the surface. After everyone in the class has moved one photon from the center to the surface find the class average of the number of rolls required.

Record the results:

Number of rolls needed to leave the surface _____

Class average of rolls needed to leave surface _____

5 results

Mathematicians can show that the average for many such photons should be close to N^2 where N is the number of layers in the diagram. Since there are 10 layers in this diagram the average should be about 100.

The Sun and stars are three-dimensional objects and the process is more complicated in them, but even in these objects there is an average number of collisions in the life of photons leaving the object. Since photons all move at the speed of light, this means that there is an average time that most photons take to escape from the interior of a star. For the Sun this time is about 5000 to 10,000 years. Thus most of the light we see coming from the Sun was produced at the Sun's center some 5000 years or more ago.

6 different stars

Using Figure 27–1 as a pattern, draw a diagram that has only four layers. This might be thought of as a smaller star. Starting photons at the center, move them to the surface. Count the number of rolls needed for the photon to escape from the surface of the star. Do this for at least 5 photons and record the average number of interactions below.

Average number of rolls needed to leave the surface _____

We know from mathematics that the average of a large number of trials should be about 16 rolls. This might lead us to suspect that in smaller stars the light can escape more quickly. In fact many things affect the flow of energy in a star, such as density and temperature. In addition many stars have regions where energy is carried by convection, the boiling motion of hot gases rising upward and cool gases sinking downward.

opacity
(a game of photons)

1 materials

One die.

2 purpose

This game demonstrates some of the ways in which starlight interacts with clouds of gas. It shows how absorption lines form in the spectra of stars and how emission nebulae radiate light.

3 light and matter

Photons of light can be absorbed by an atom if the photon has the correct amount of energy to move an electron from one orbit to another. Later when the electron spontaneously returns to its lower orbit the photon is re-radiated in a new random direction. Thus, each time the photon is absorbed by an atom its path is changed in a random way.

In this exercise we imagine a source of photons and a cloud of gas. The cloud could be a nebula near a star, or it could be the atmosphere of the star itself. In any case the light will be affected as it passes through the cloud on its way from the surface of the star to our telescope. If the gas absorbs photons easily it will be difficult for the light to get through the cloud and we would say the cloud is opaque. The opacity is a measure of how opaque the gas is.

4 playing opacity

The game board shown in Figure 28–1 is a two-dimensional representation of a cloud of gas. Light from the surface of a star enters the cloud from the upper left and strikes the atom numbered 1. In this game if a photon is

179

absorbed, there are only six directions it can go when it is reradiated. To select randomly the direction of reradiation, roll the die and multiply the number that comes up by 2. The result is the clock face direction 2, 4, 6, 8, 10, or 12 o'clock as shown in the small figure to the upper right. We will assume that any photon that leaves the cloud traveling in the 4 o'clock direction will reach our telescope and is counted a success. A photon that leaves the cloud in any other direction will never reach our telescope and is counted a failure.

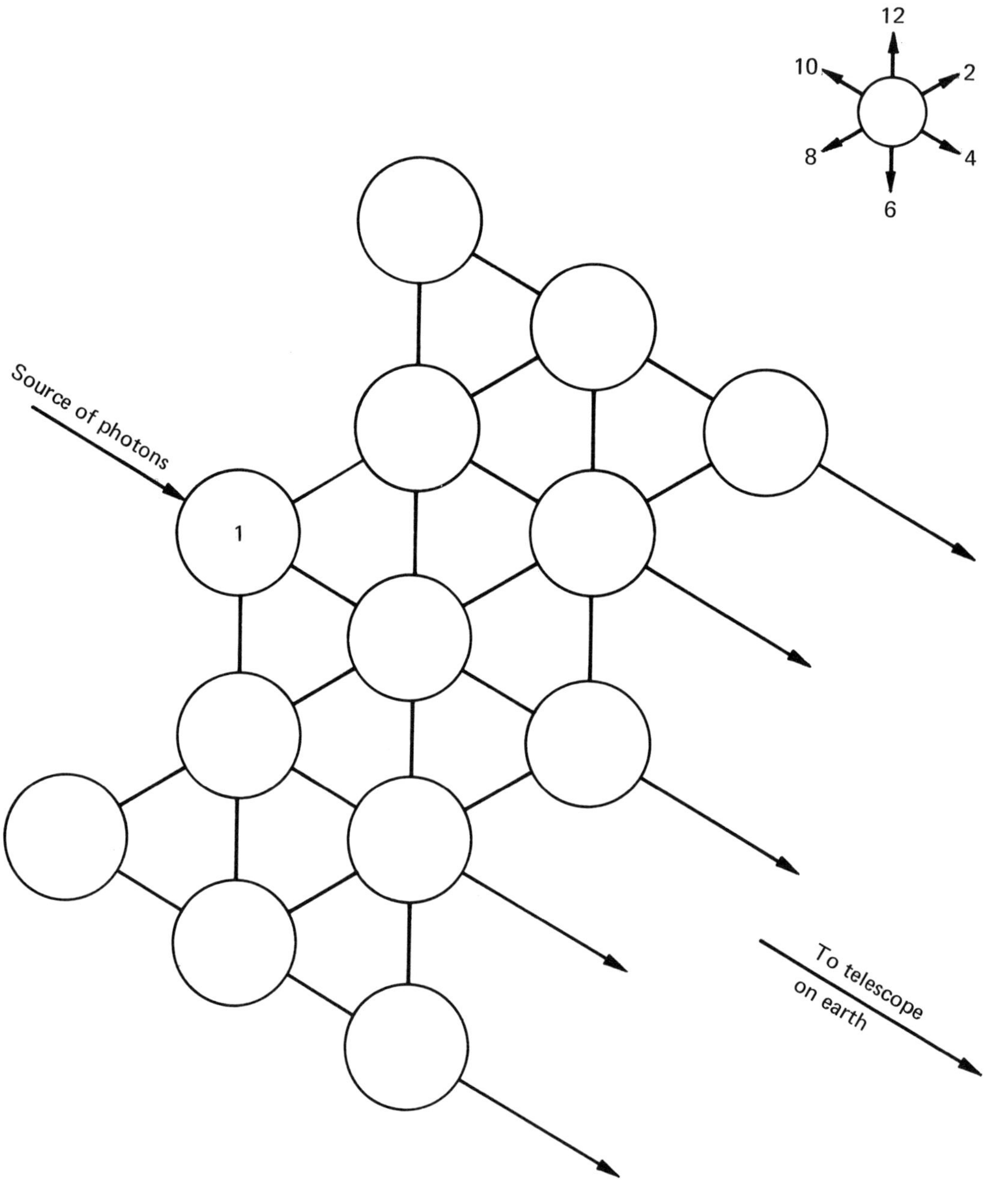

Figure 28-1. Game board for playing Opacity. Each circle represents a particle in a cloud of gas.

stars

5 solitaire opacity

Using a penny as a marker try to move ten photons, one at a time, through the cloud. Each photon must interact with every atom it encounters. These photons have a wavelength and an energy that the atoms easily affect and are called **line radiation photons**. Keep track of your successes and failures.

activity

movement of line radiation photons

Number of successes: _____ (photons leaving cloud in 4 o'clock direction).

Number of failures: _____ (photons leaving cloud in other directions).

If a photon has an energy that does not interact easily with the atoms it should be easier for the photon to get through the gas. Such photons are called **continuum photons**. Although continuum photons do not get absorbed by atoms, they may be scattered by encounters with atoms and electrons.

activity

Read Section 3 of Exercise 27, The Flow of Energy Out of the Sun, and write a short description of the kinds of scattering processes we might expect in a thin cloud of cool gas.

To play the game with continuum photons, we must follow a photon as it moves through the cloud of gas. Each time the photon encounters a particle we must decide in some random way whether the photon will be scattered or whether it will continue on its way undisturbed. To make this random decision we will roll our die. If a 6 comes up we will say the photon has been scattered. If any number other than a 6 comes up we will say that no scattering occurred, and we will move our photon on in the direction it was traveling before it encountered the atom. In our game continuum photons will be scattered in about one out of six encounters.

If the photon is scattered, we must then decide randomly on its new direction of travel. We do this by rolling the die again and following the clock face direction as described earlier.

Play ten continuum photons through the cloud and keep track of successes and failures. Remember, if the photon is not scattered, move it on in the direction it was traveling before it encountered the particle.

activity

movement of continuum radiation photons

Number of successes: _____ (photons leaving cloud in 4 o'clock direction).

Number of failures: _____ (photons leaving cloud in other directions).

6 what it means

Notice that very few if any of the line radiation photons were able to get through the cloud. These photons are too easily absorbed and reradiated. If on Earth we used a filter to admit only these line photons to our telescope, we would not be able to see the star through the gas. The gas would be opaque. Astronomers would say the gas was optically thick to the line radiation. However, if we look at the continuum photons, we would be able to see the star through the gas. The gas would be optically thin to the continuum radiation.

Whether a cloud of gas is optically thick or optically thin depends on how susceptible the photons are to interaction with the atoms of the gas. This depends mostly on the wavelength of the photons.

This effect can be used in the study of the solar surface. The Sun's atmosphere is a cloud of gas, so if an astronomer uses a special device to filter out everything except photons in the hydrogen alpha line, or the calcium K line (both strong lines in the solar spectrum) he will be unable to see very deep into the Sun's atmosphere. It would be optically thick. But photographs taken in this way show the details of what is happening high in the atmosphere of the Sun. If we look at the Sun using continuum photons, the atmosphere is optically thin and we look through the atmosphere to the photosphere below. In your text book see if you can find some hydrogen alpha or calcium K line filtergrams of the Sun.

7   emission and absorption spectra

An atom can only absorb photons with just the right energies. Since energy depends on wavelength, this means that an atom can only absorb photons with just the right wavelengths. We have called these photons line radiation because if we attach a spectrograph to our telescope and point it at the star behind the gas cloud, we will get a spectrum with dark lines. Those photons with just the right energies do not get through the cloud very easily and do not enter our telescope. In our spectrum at the corresponding wavelengths we see dark lines. But the photons that do not get absorbed by atoms are able to get through the cloud rather easily and reach our telescope in great numbers. Their part of the spectrum, the spaces between the dark lines, are bright. Such a spectrum with a bright continuum and dark lines is called an absorption spectrum or a dark line spectrum.

If we point our telescope to one side, away from the star, and look only at the gas cloud, we would see very few continuum photons because most of them go straight through the cloud. But we would see a number of line photons, since they are absorbed and reradiated most easily. Then the spectrum of the gas alone would be dark with bright lines at the wavelengths of the line photons. This is an emission spectrum, also called a bright line spectrum.

If there were no lines in the spectrum and all wavelength photons were present, the spectrum would be smooth, featureless, and continuous. This kind of spectrum is called a continuous spectrum. Since every star is surrounded by a cloud of gas called its atmosphere, continuous spectra do not normally occur in stellar spectra.

8   supplement on optical depth

It is common in astronomy to refer to the thickness of a cloud of gas not in miles but in terms of its optical depth. Optical depth is a measure of how many photons are able to get through the gas. If F_i represents the flux of light entering the cloud, and F_o represents the flux of light that emerges from the other side then the optical depth τ is defined by

$$F_o = F_i \, e^{-\tau}$$

If we think of F_i as the number of photons that enter the cloud and F_o as the number that get through, then F_o divided by F_i is the fraction of photons that get through. Call this fraction S. Then our formula becomes

$$e^{-\tau} = S = \frac{F_o}{F_i}.$$

If we take the logarithm of both sides we get

$$\tau = -\ln S. \qquad (28\text{-}1)$$

The table below shows values of τ for various values of S as calculated by formula (28-1).

$S = F_o/F_i$	τ
0.0	—
0.05	3.00
0.1	2.30
0.2	1.61
0.3	1.20
0.4	0.92
0.5	0.69
0.6	0.51
0.7	0.36
0.8	0.22
0.9	0.11
1.0	0.00

Refer to your results in Section 5 of this exercise and complete the table below for the two kinds of photons we have considered.

	$S = F_o/F_i$	τ
Continum		
Line		

Notice that the cloud of gas is optically thicker in the line than in the continuum.

Optical thickness, τ, depends not only on the wavelength, but also on the density of the atoms and the distance through the cloud. If the cloud is of very low density, say 1 atom/cm^3 it might still be optically thick if the light has to travel many light years through the cloud. And even if the gas cloud is only 1 cm across, it may be optically thick if the density is very high.

The optical thickness also depends on the kind of atoms involved because different atoms absorb different wavelengths. For any given type of atom under given conditions there is a number called the opacity that represents the ability of the gas to interact with photons of given wavelength. Opacity depends on wavelength. It is a measure of how "sticky" the gas atoms are for certain photons.

Since opacity is a function of wavelength, so also is τ dependent on wavelength. Thus the ease with which photons can move through the cloud of gas depends on the wavelength of the photons, the kind of gas, the density and temperature of the gas, and the width of the cloud.

Name _____

Section _____ Date _____

spectral classification

1 materials   None.

2 purpose   This exercise will introduce you to stellar spectra. You will have an opportunity to study some of the features of the spectra and to classify some of the stars.

3 stellar spectra   Study Figure 29–1. This photograph was made with an objective prism in front of the telescope lens. As a result each star produces an objective prism spectrum. Notice that each spectrum is crossed by dark lines. Some have many lines, and some have only a few. These features are clues to the temperature of the star.

     The inset in the lower left corner of Figure 29–1 is a guide to the features in these spectra. Trace this template on the edge of a slip of paper so you can place it directly under the various spectra to aid in the identification of the lines.

4 spectral classification   Stars are classified into a number of classes which are lettered O, B, A, F, G, K, M. This sequence can be remembered by the mnemonic "Oh Be A Fine Girl, Kiss Me." This sequence is a temperature sequence running from the hottest stars, the O stars, to the coolest stars, the M stars. The approximate temperatures of stars of these classes are given in Table 29–1.

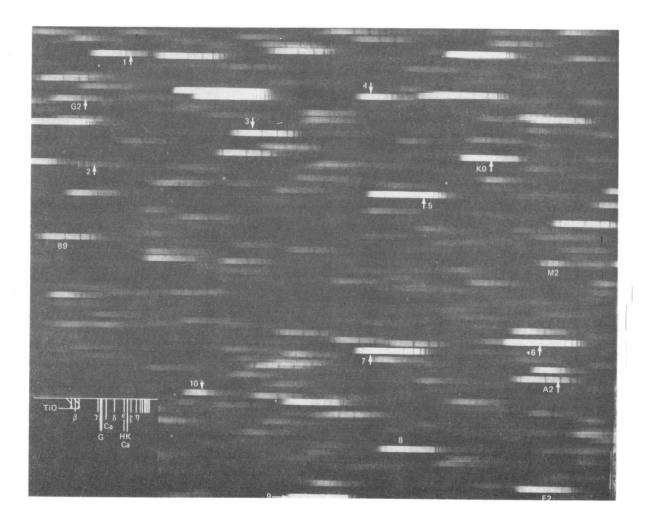

Figure 29-1. Objective prism spectra of stars near the southern Milky Way. [Courtesy of Department of Astronomy, University of Michigan]

Notice in Table 29–1 that subclasses are used so that a star intermediate between G and K might be called a G5 star. The sun is not quite this cool and is classified as a G2 star. Generally there are ten subdivisions of a class, for example, F0, F1, ..., F9.

Use the template you have made to examine the spectrum labeled B9. This star is rather hot and nearly all the atoms in its atmosphere have been ionized; that is, the atoms have lost one or more electrons. There are very few lines in this spectrum as compared with the spectrum of the G2 star. The G2 star is cooler, so the gases are less ionized and more lines appear in its spectrum.

The lines in the B9 spectrum are the Balmer lines of hydrogen. From left to right they are β, γ, δ, ϵ, ζ, η, and so on. The Balmer a line is not visible in these spectra because it is in the red part of the spectrum. The spectra go from the blue-green on the left to the ultraviolet on the right. The wavelengths of the Balmer lines are given in Table 29–2. Place a check mark beside those lines you can see in the spectrum of the B9 star.

Table 29-1 Temperatures of Stars

Spectral Type	Temperature ($^\circ K$)
05	35,000
B0	21,000
B5	14,000
A0	9,800
A5	8,000
F0	7,200
F5	6,500
G0	6,000
G5	5,400
K0	4,700
K5	4,000
M0	3,200
M5	2,500

Table 29-2 Wavelengths of the Balmer Lines

Line	Wavelength (Å)
α	6563
β	4861
γ	4340
δ	4102
ϵ	3970
ζ	3889
η	3835
θ	3798

The A2 star is slightly cooler than the B9 star. The F2 star is even cooler. Use the template to locate the G band and the calcium line at 4226Å. The G band is a mixture of lines produced by the molecule CH (methylidine) and various atoms such as iron. The calcium 4226 Å line is caused by un-ionized calcium. These features are not present in the spectra of hot stars because the CN molecule is easily dissociated and calcium is easily ionized at high temperatures.

activity

Can you detect the G band or the Ca 4226 line in the spectrum of the B9 star?

Examine the spectrum of the F2 star in Figure 29-1 and locate the H and K lines of singly ionized calcium. The H line nearly coincides with the Balmer ϵ line and the K line falls about halfway between ϵ and ζ. Try to find the H and K lines in the spectrum of the A2 star.

activity

Why would we expect the H and K lines to be weak in the spectra of hot stars?

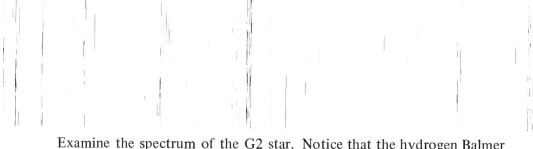

Examine the spectrum of the G2 star. Notice that the hydrogen Balmer lines are quite weak and that the G band and the H and K lines of calcium are very strong. There is lots of hydrogen present in the atmosphere of the star, but the temperature is so low that most of the hydrogen atoms have their electrons in their lowest orbit. Balmer absorption lines only form when the electron makes transitions from the second orbit to outer orbits. Thus in cool stars the Balmer lines are weak. Compare the G2 spectrum with the K0 spectrum. Notice how weak the Balmer lines are and that there are many lines in these cool star spectra.

Now examine the spectrum of the M2 star. Notice that the calcium 4226 line has become the strongest line in the spectrum. The G band is weaker in these very cool stars.

Titanium oxide, TiO, is a molecule that forms when the temperature of a star is very low. This molecule produces bands of lines on either side of the Balmer β line. Locate these bands and notice that they are sharp on the right and are shaded to the left.

5 classification of stars

It is now possible to classify the spectra of the stars in Figure 29-1. To classify a spectrum, first decide if it shows few lines and is therefore hot, or shows many lines and is therefore cool. If it is hot look for the K line of calcium. If in these spectra the K line is invisible or just visible, it is a B or A star. If the K line seems strong look for the G band. The G band becomes visible at about A2 and is strongest at about G5 to K0. If the star is cool look for the Ca 4226 line and compare it with the G band. In these spectra, the G band and the Ca 4226 line will seem equal in intensity at about K5.

If TiO bands are visible, the star is an M star. These bands get stronger as you go from M0 to M5 and the G band gets weaker. As you work keep comparing the unclassified star with the classified stars.

Study the ten numbered spectra and classify them as accurately as you can. Then estimate their temperatures from Table 29–1. Record your results in Table 29–3. Later your instructor will provide you with the accepted classifications of these stars so you may check your work. If you come within a few subclasses you are doing fine.

Table 29-3 Classification of Stars

Star	Class	Temperature
1	_____	_____
2	_____	_____
3	_____	_____
4	_____	_____
5	_____	_____
6	_____	_____
7	_____	_____
8	_____	_____
9	_____	_____
10	_____	_____

optional questions

1. Why are there more lines in cool stars than in hot stars?

2. Why are the hydrogen Balmer lines weaker in the cooler stars?

3. Why do the hydrogen Balmer lines get closer and closer together at shorter wavelengths?

4. In what ways do the TiO bands differ from the G band?

5. Why might we expect the hydrogen Balmer lines to be weak in very hot stars?

6. If we do not see lines of a specific element in a star's spectrum, may we conclude that that element is absent? Why?

exercise

30

the H-R diagram

1 materials

Straight edge.

2 purpose

This exercise will permit you to explore the family relations among the stars in the sky by using H-R Diagrams. An H-R diagram is a plot of the absolute magnitudes of stars against their spectral types. You will discover that there are many different kinds of stars of different brightness, surface temperature, and size. These properties of stars are not immediately apparent to the casual observer.

3 the main sequence

Plot all of the stars in Table 30–1 on Figure 30–1. Sketch a smooth curve through the points. This curve is called the **main sequence** because most stars fall on this line. The diagram is known as an H-R diagram in honor of Hertzsprung and Russell who discovered the relation between absolute magnitude and spectral type.

Stars are grouped into six luminosity classes denoted by the Roman numerals Ia, Ib, II, III, IV, V. Stars that fall on the main sequence are classed as luminosity class V stars, and the spectral types are written with Roman numeral V, as in G2V for the Sun. Add a V to each of the spectral types in Table 30–1. We know that all main sequence stars are burning hydrogen at their centers. The main sequence is the line of hydrogen burning stars. Now add the stars in Table 30–2 to Figure 30–1 and draw a small oval around them.

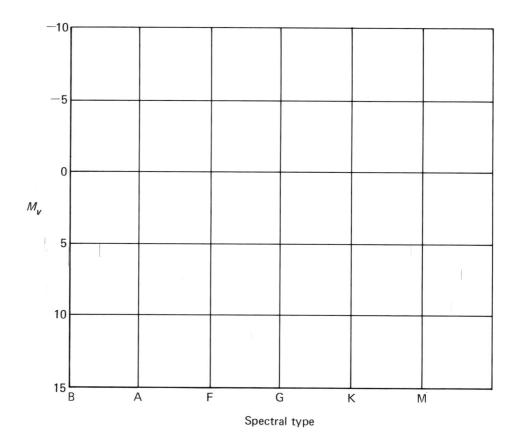

Figure 30-1. H-R diagram form for use with Tables 30-1 and 30-2.

Table 30–1 Main Sequence Stars

Star	Type	M_v
Sun	G2	+5.0
σ Per A	B0	−3.7
γ Cet	A2	+2.0
α Hyi	F0	+2.9
Kruger 60B	M6	+13.2
Procyon A	F5	+2.7
61 Cyg A	K5	+7.5
τ Cet	G8	+5.7
α Gru	B5	+0.3
Kapteyn's Star	M0	+10.8

Table 30-2 Giant Stars

Star	Type	M_v
Arcturus	K2	−0.3
Capella	G2	+0.0
Aldebaran	K5	−0.7
Pollux	K0	+1.0

question

Why don't these stars lie on the main sequence?

4 giants and dwarfs

The stars in Table 30-2 are called giants, and their spectral types are written with a III, such as K2III. Add III's to the spectral types in Table 30-2. The list of luminosity classes is given as follows:

Luminosity Class	Type of Star
Ia and Ib	Supergiants
II	Bright giants
III	Giants
IV	Subgiants
V	Dwarfs (main sequence stars)

Notice that the Sun is a dwarf star. Sometimes class V stars are called main sequence dwarfs to distinguish them from the white dwarfs which do not fit into this luminosity classification scheme.

Are giants really bigger than dwarfs? Since Capella is a G2 star we know that it has the same surface temperature as the Sun, another G2 star. Consequently each star gives off the same amount and color of light from each square centimeter of surface. But Capella is more luminous than the sun, so it must have more surface area radiating energy.

1. How many magnitudes is Capella brighter than the Sun? _____

2. How many times brighter is Capella than the Sun? _____

3. How many times more surface area has Capella than the Sun? _____

4. How does the radius of Capella compare with that of the Sun? (*Hint*: The area of a sphere is $4\pi R^2$.) _____

Stars such as Capella are called giants because of their size.

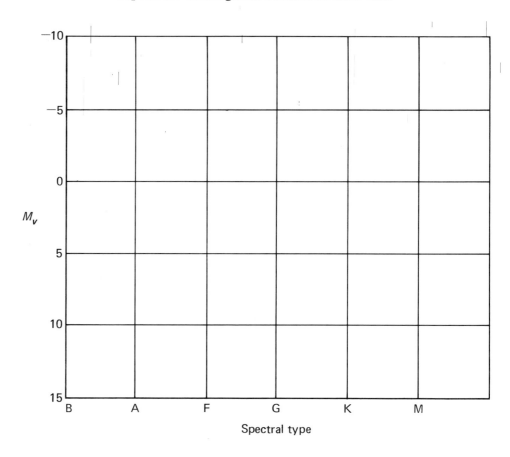

Figure 30-2. H–R diagram form for use with Table 30-3.

5 **the brightest stars in the sky** In Figure 30–2 plot all of the stars from Table 30–3. Transfer the main sequence from Figure 30–1 to Figure 30–2.

Table 30-3 The brightest stars

Star	m_v	M_v	Type
Sirius	−1.4	1.5	A1V
Canopus	−0.7	−4.0	F0Ib
Rigil Kentaurus	−0.3	4.4	G2V
Arcturus	−0.1	−0.3	K2III
Vega	0.0	0.5	A0V
Capella	0.1	0.0	G2III
Rigel	0.1	−7.1	B8Ia
Procyon	0.4	2.7	F5IV–V
Betelgeuse	0.4	−5.6	M2Ia
Achernar	0.5	−3.0	B5IV
Hadar	0.6	−3.0	B1II
Altair	0.8	2.3	A7IV–V
Acrux	0.8	−3.9	B1IV
Aldebaran	0.9	−0.7	K5III
Antares	0.9	−3.0	M1Ib
Spica	0.9	−2.0	B1V
Pollux	1.2	1.0	K0III
Fomalhaut	1.2	2.0	A3V
Deneb	1.3	−7.1	A2Ia
Beta Crucis	1.3	−4.6	B0III
Regulus	1.4	−0.6	B7V
Adhara	1.5	−5.1	B2II
Castor	1.6	0.9	A1V
Shaula	1.6	−3.3	B1V
Bellatrix	1.6	−2.0	B2III
Elnath	1.7	−3.2	B7III
Miaplacidus	1.7	−0.4	A0III
Alnilam	1.7	−6.8	B0Ia

questions

1. What is the most common kind of bright star? (hot/cool) _____

2. Estimate the average apparent magnitude of these stars from the table.

   _____

3. When you look at a bright, 1st magnitude star in the sky, you are probably looking at a_____ star.

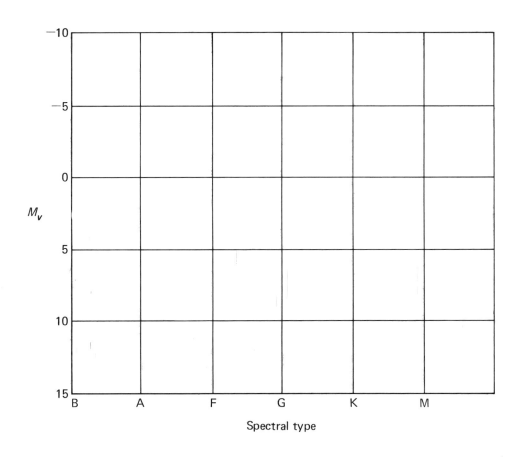

Figure 30-3. H-R diagram form for use with Table 30-4.

6 the nearest stars

Plot all of the stars from Table 30–4 on Figure 30–3. These are the stars that are near the Sun in space. Since we believe that the Sun is in an ordinary part of our galaxy, we must conclude that these stars are common, ordinary stars.

questions

1. What is the most common kind of star near the Sun? (hot/cool) _____

2. Estimate the average apparent magnitude of these stars from the table.

_____

The bright stars that we see in the sky are rather far away. But we see them because they are intrinsically very bright. An ordinary star is rather faint, and even though there are many near the Sun we do not see them easily because they are not very luminous.

Table 30–4 The Nearest Stars

Star	m_v	M_v	Spectral Type
Sun	−26.8	4.8	G2
Proxima Centauri	11.0	15.4	M5
Alpha Centauri A	0.1	4.4	G2
Alpha Centauri B	1.5	5.8	K5
Barnard's Star	9.5	13.2	M5
Wolf 359	13.5	16.7	M6
Lalande 21185	7.5	10.5	M2
Sirius A	− 1.4	1.5	A1
Sirius B	7.2	10.1	wd
Luyten 726–8A	12.5	15.3	M6
Luyten 726–8B	13.0	15.8	M6
Ross 154	10.6	13.3	M5
Epsilon Eridani	3.7	6.1	K2
Luyten 789–6	12.2	14.6	M6
Ross 128	11.1	13.5	M5
61 Cygni A	5.2	7.5	K5
61 Cygni B	6.0	8.3	K7
Epsilon Indi	4.7	7.0	K5
Procyon A	0.3	2.7	F5
Procyon B	10.8	13.1	wd
Cincinnati 2456A	8.9	11.2	M4
Cincinnati 2456B	9.7	12.0	M4
Groombridge 34A	8.1	10.4	M1
Groombridge 34B	11.0	13.3	M6
Lacaille 9352	7.4	9.6	M2
Tau Ceti	3.5	5.7	G8
Luyten's Star	9.8	11.9	M4
Lacaille 8760	6.7	8.8	M1
Kapteyn's Star	8.8	10.8	M0
Kruger 60A	9.7	11.7	M4
Kruger 60B	11.2	13.2	M6

questions

1. What would our night sky look like if all the stars in our galaxy had the same absolute magnitude as the Sun?

2. Would we see more stars or fewer stars? Why?

3. Would we see more 1st magnitude stars or fewer? Why?

exercise

31

the H-R diagram for NGC 6819

1 materials   None.

2 purpose   This exercise will permit you to make measurements of star images on a photograph of a cluster and then plot an H-R diagram of the cluster. The H-R diagram of a cluster is important because it permits you to determine the distance to the cluster, its age, and the possible presence of interstellar matter between you and the cluster.

3 stellar photometry   In order to obtain the H-R diagram of a cluster it is necessary to measure the apparent brightness and color of the individual stars in the cluster. This is called stellar photometry and can be done in two ways. We can photograph the cluster and measure the brightness of individual stars from the photograph by measuring the sizes of their images, or we can photometer the stars one by one at the telescope photoelectrically. This photoelectric approach is the most accurate, but it consumes large amounts of telescope time. It takes a total of 10 to 30 minutes to observe a single star, and telescope time is too valuable to be used in this way. The photographic method is less accurate, but in a few hours an astronomer can take photographic plates of a cluster and record the brightness and color of hundreds of stars. It is good practice then to measure a few stars photoelectrically and use them as standard stars to calibrate the photographic plate. This is the procedure we will follow.

In order to measure the colors of stars, astronomers measure the magnitudes of the stars through colored filters. The V magnitude is a visual magnitude and is measured through a yellow filter with a wavelength of about

5480 Å. The B magnitude is a blue magnitude measured through a blue filter with a wavelength of about 4400 Å. The color index of a star is the difference of these two magnitudes, which is written simply B-V. If the star is very red it will be fainter in B than in V and B-V will be positive; if the star is very blue it will be fainter in V than in B and B-V will be negative. The more positive the B-V index, the redder the star.

The photographic plates can be taken through blue and yellow filters and different kinds of emulsions can be used that are sensitive to different parts of the spectrum. In this way it is possible to obtain a V plate and a B plate of a cluster. Then, by comparison of the images of the stars in the cluster with the images of the standard stars on the same plate, we can determine the V magnitude and the B magnitude for all the stars. If V is plotted versus B-V, we will obtain an observational H-R diagram, or, as it is frequently called, a color-magnitude diagram.

4 measuring the plate

At the observatory the astronomer would measure the size of each star image on a special machine. Since these machines are quite large and expensive, we must get along without one. Fortunately it is quite easy to measure the diameters of star images with a simple wedge scale. The wedge scale drawn in Figure 31–1 should be traced on thin paper or plastic so that, as the scale is placed over a photograph of stars, you can measure the images through the wedge opening.

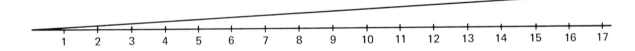

Figure 31-1. Wedge scale for measuring diameters of star images in Figure 31-2.

Since we must measure many stars in this rather crude way, we will reduce part of the work by measuring only one plate. We will assume that someone else has determined the B-V colors for all of the stars for us. These B-V values are given in Table 31–1 with space for us to enter our results as we measure the V plate shown in Figure 31–2.

Examine Figure 31–2 and notice that this is indeed a photograph of a plate. The stars are black spots and the sky is white. Practice using the wedge scale to measure the diameters of the star images on the photograph. When you are confident you can measure stars easily, measure all of the numbered stars on the photograph, entering your data in the column marked D provided in Table 31–1. Measure D to the nearest tenth of a unit.

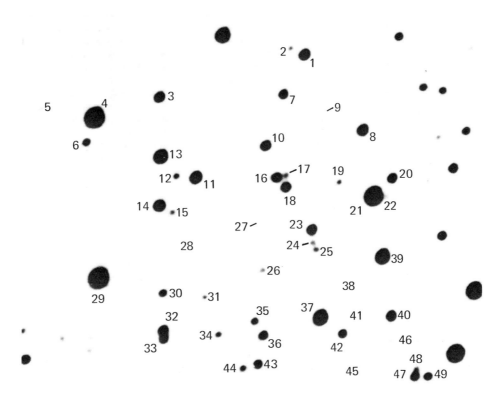

Figure 31-2. Reproduction of photographic plate of star cluster NGC 6819. [Courtesy of Martin S. Burkhead, Indiana University.]

Table 31-1 Photometric Data

Star	D	V	B-V	Star	D	V	B-V
1			0.58	25			0.90
2			0.77	26			0.77
3			0.59	27		17.90	1.10
4			1.21	28			0.87
5		17.06	0.98	30			0.64
6		15.97	0.62	31		16.69	0.74
7			0.66	32			0.62
8			1.16	33			0.46
9			1.37	34			0.69
10		15.03	0.58	35			0.62
11		13.97	1.12	36			0.55
12			0.73	37			1.09
13		13.29	1.25	38			0.98
14			0.46	39			1.05
15			0.73	40			0.65
16			0.49	41			1.02
18			0.54	42			0.59
19			0.70	43			0.50
20			0.55	44			0.67
21		12.87	0.11	45			1.05
22			0.70	47			0.48
23			0.50	48			0.59
24			0.67	49			0.49

5 the calibration curve

The measurements you have made give the diameters of the star images in some arbitrary unit. To convert these to magnitudes, plot in Figure 31-3 your measurements versus the known magnitudes for all of the stars listed with known V. These are the standard stars and through them we can find the relation between image diameter and magnitude. This relationship is the calibration curve. Sketch a smooth curve through the points in the graph.

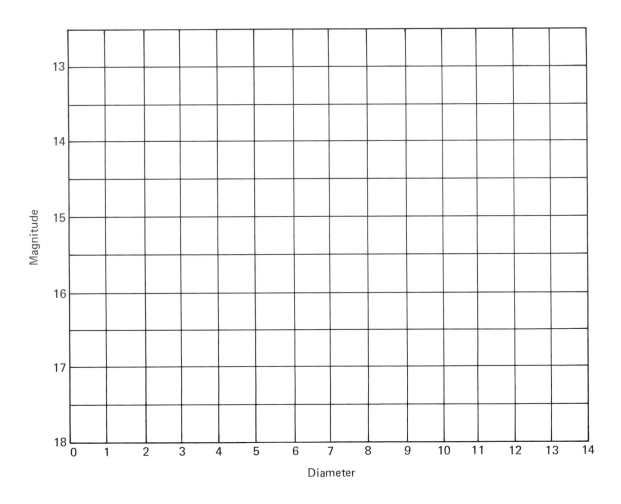

Figure 31-3. Calibration curve form for the standard stars in Figure 31-2.

Take the measured diameter of a star from the table, use the calibration curve to convert this diameter to a magnitude, and write the magnitude in Table 31–1 in the column provided. Since the plate was a V plate, these are V magnitudes.

the h-r diagram for ngc 6819

6 **the color-magnitude diagram**

The color-magnitude diagram can now be plotted in Figure 31–4. Plot the B-V values and apparent magnitudes of all of the stars from Table 31–1 including the standard stars.

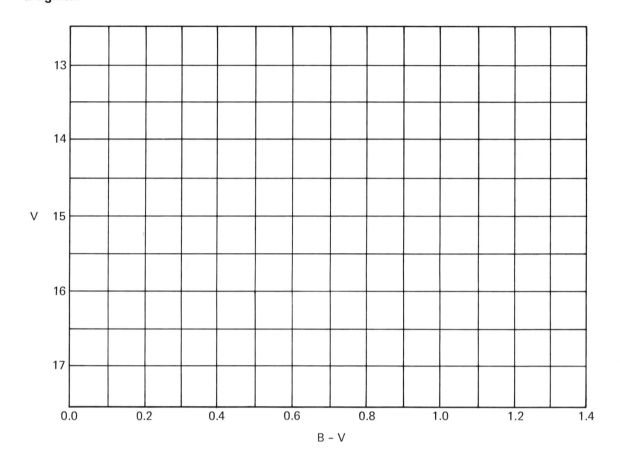

Figure 31-4. Form for color-magnitude diagram of stars in NGC 6819.

Since this is a galactic cluster you will find a short main sequence and a few giant stars. Sketch in a line for the main sequence of the cluster. Table 31–2 contains the B-V values and absolute magnitudes of the main sequence of hydrogen burning stars. The main sequence of the cluster appears fainter in apparent magnitude because it is further away than the standard distance of 10 parsecs. From your color-magnitude diagram determine the magnitude of the cluster main sequence at as many of the indicated B-V values as possible. Enter these data under V (cluster) in Table 31–2. The distance modulus is the difference $V - M_v$ where M_v is the absolute visual magnitude of the main sequence. Calculate these differences and average them to find the distance modulus of the cluster.

The distance modulus is the difference between the apparent magnitude and the absolute magnitude of the main sequence stars in the cluster. This difference depends only on the distance to the cluster and is related to distance by the formula

$$V - M_v = 5 \log (d) - 5$$

where d is the distance to the cluster in parsecs, and V is visual magnitude used in place of the more common notation m.

Use your distance modulus to calculate the distance to the cluster in parsecs.

$$d = \underline{\hspace{3cm}} \text{ parsecs.}$$

Notice that the accuracy of the number you have just calculated depends not only on how well we have measured magnitudes and colors but also on how well we know the data in columns 1 and 2 of Table 31–2. The data given there is based on the cluster in Taurus called the Hyades. The distance to the Hyades can be determined in a number of independent ways and is thus rather well known; it is, indeed, the basic calibration of the position of the main sequence in the H-R diagram. There is still some debate as to the true distance to the Hyades. If the distance is wrong, then the absolute magnitudes given in Table 31–2 are wrong, and most of the distances in astronomy are wrong. Thus the distance modulus of the Hyades cluster is one of the most important numbers in astronomy.

Table 31–2

B-V	M_v	V (cluster)	V-M_v (distance modulus)
0.00	1.50		
0.20	2.50		
0.40	3.60		
0.60	4.80		
0.80	5.90		

Average distance modulus = \underline{\hspace{3cm}}

7   the age of the cluster It is possible to find the distance to the cluster because all of the stars are at about the same distance from us. It is also possible to determine the age of the cluster, because all of the stars were born at about the same time and are thus all of about the same age. The stars all formed from the same cloud of material and so have the same initial composition, but some were very massive stars and some were very low mass stars. We know that massive stars burn their fuel quickly, are very hot, blue and bright, and do not live very long. Low mass stars are cool, red and faint, and have very long life expectancies.

Examination of your color-magnitude diagram will show that the bright blue portion of the main sequence is missing. Evidently the cluster is old enough for all of the massive stars to have evolved off the main sequence and ended their lives in whatever way they were destined. Notice that one star does lie on the bright blue main sequence. Perhaps it does not belong to the cluster, or perhaps for some reason it has remained behind while its hot and very luminous blue companions have died. Such stars are called blue stragglers and no one really understands them. Perhaps they are the result of the peculiar evolution of close binary stars.

It is evident that this cluster is not young, but how old is it? That can only be answered if we know how long it takes for a star to evolve and how it will move in the color-magnitude diagram when it leaves the main sequence. Studies of mathematical models of stars of different masses have been made, and the result of these studies is summarized in Figure 31-5.

Here the main sequence is shown along with a number of lines called isochrons. Imagine that a cluster of stars was born with stars of all different masses starting their lives at exactly the same time. After a given period of time some stars would have died completely, others would have moved into the red giant region, and still others would be just leaving the main sequence. They would thus draw a line of constant time in the color-magnitude diagram, an isochron. The isochrons in the graph indicate age in billions of years. The older a cluster is the further toward the red (greater B-V) it will turn off from the main sequence.

Lay a blank sheet of paper over Figure 31-5 and trace the axes, main sequence, and isochrons. Lay this tracing on top of Figure 31-4 and slide it up and down keeping the left edges of the figures aligned and match the main sequence of the tracing to the main sequence of the cluster. Examine the cluster and the isochrons.

problems

1. Which isochron best represents the shape and turn off point of the cluster? If necessary estimate between isochrons to determine the age of the

   cluster. Age = _____ billion years.

Such age determinations depend strongly on the theoretical models which are very sensitive to the initial composition of the stars. Thus it is only an approximation to the age of the cluster, but we can see that this cluster is very old indeed. It is one of the oldest clusters known.

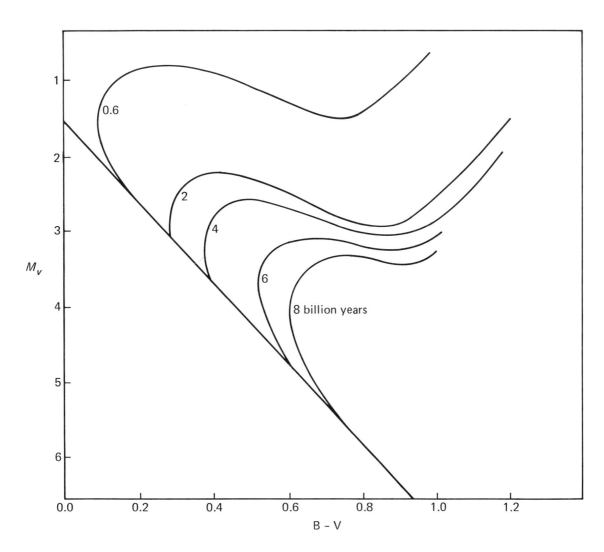

Figure 31-5. Main sequence and isochrons for theoretical clusters of different ages.

2. If the Sun were a member of the cluster, where would it be in the color-magnitude diagram? Plot its position by calculating the apparent magnitude of the sun at the distance of the cluster. For the Sun, $M_v = 4.79$ and B-V = 0.62.

supplementary problems

If interstellar material is present in the form of gas and dust between us and the cluster, it can reduce the brightness of the stars and make them redder. Suppose this material is present and that the data in Table 31–1 are 0.1 magnitudes too red (B–V) and 0.3 magnitudes too faint (V).

1. Then what is the correct distance to the cluster? _____

2. How does this affect the age of the cluster?

Students may enjoy consulting the original paper on which this exercise is based. "Photometric Observation of the Star Cluster NGC 6819" by Martin S. Burkhead, 1971 *Astronomical Journal* Vol. 76, page 251.

Nova Serpentis 1970

1 materials

None.

2 purpose

On February 13, 1970, Honda, an observer in Japan, discovered a nova. Observatories around the world were notified by telegram and observation began immediately. This exercise will allow you to share in some of the work that went on at that time. You will be able to reproduce one of the discoveries that was made in the days following the discovery of the nova.

3 the light curve

The nova was observed by many astronomers around the world and some of their data are reproduced in Table 32-1. The apparent visual magnitude is given for the Greenwich date of the observation. The date listed is a decimal day representing the date and approximate time. Thus 13.8 corresponds to about 19:00 hours on the 13th. In plotting the data it is best to leave the dates in the decimal day form.

Table 32-1

Date	m_v	Date	m_v
Feb. 13.8	7.00	Feb. 22.4	4.69
15.8	5.00	24.4	4.63
16.8	4.70	26.4	4.77
17.8	4.56	Mar. 5.2	5.40
18.5	4.42	7.2	5.50
20.4	4.61	10.2	5.60
21.4	4.62	12.2	5.80

Plot these data in Figure 32–1. This represents the "light curve" of the nova. It began faint, became bright, and then gradually faded. Keeping in mind that the data are subject to small errors that may produce some scatter, sketch a smooth curve through these points to represent your best estimate of the true light curve of the nova.

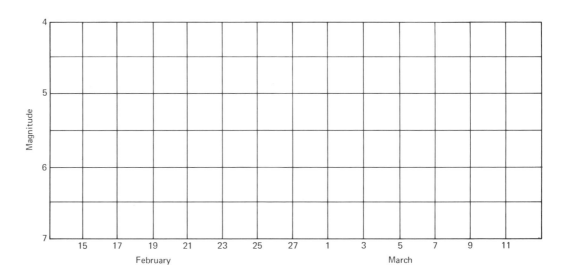

Figure 32-1. Diagram for the light curve of Nova Serpentis 1970.

activity

1. On what decimal date did the nova reach its brightest? _____

2. Estimate its magnitude at brightest.

   $m_v = $ _____   •

3. In Figure 32–1 brightness increases in going from the bottom of the vertical scale to the top. Why is the magnitude scale seemingly reversed?

4. What is a nova? Look it up and describe its appearance and possible cause in a few sentences.

4 the prenova

No one knows how to predict which of the billions of stars in our galaxy are about to become novae. But once the star becomes a nova, we can no longer tell what kind of star it used to be, unless we can find it on an earlier photograph. This is one of the reasons why a complete photographic record of the sky was made in the 1950's by the National Geographical Society and the Palomar Observatory. The Palomar Sky Survey makes it possible to search for the prenova as it appeared in the 1950's.

In an effort to identify the star that became the nova, two astronomers at Indiana University photographed the nova with a 16-in. telescope on February 26.4, 1970, 13 days after the discovery. By comparing that photograph with the Palomar Sky Survey of the area they were able to identify the prenova.

Figure 32–2 shows their photograph (lower half) and an enlargement of the Palomar Sky Survey (upper half). The photographs are negative prints so the stars appear black and the sky appears white. The large star is the nova on February 26.4, and the arrow points to the nova as it looked about 15 years earlier when the Sky Survey was made. Notice the two small star images on either side of the nova corresponding to the two stars in the upper half of the figure.

activity

From Figure 32–1 estimate the magnitude of the nova when the lower photograph was taken. $m_v = $ _____

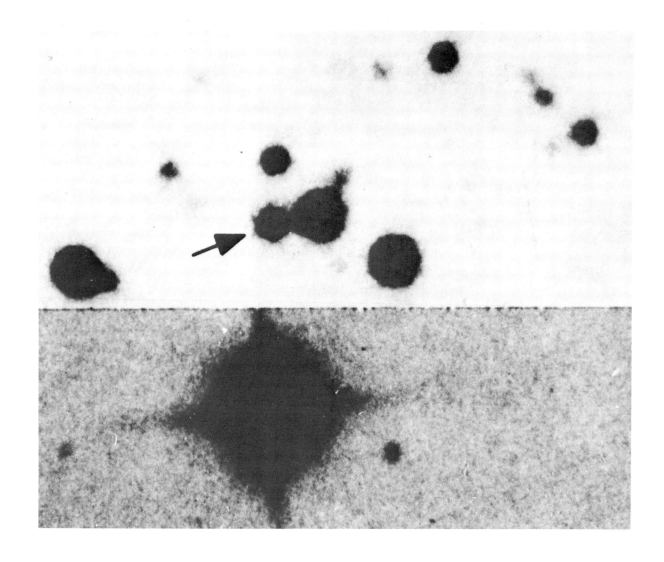

Figure 32-2. Reproduction of two plates of Nova Serpentis 1970. The arrow indicates the prenova. The large image is the nova during outburst. [M. S. Burkhead and and M. A. Seeds: *The Astrophysical Journal*, **160**: L51 (1970). Copyright by University of Chicago 1970.]

5 the magnitude of the prenova

Notice that the brighter stars have larger images. We can use this photographic effect to measure the brightness of the prenova in the upper photograph, since some of the other stars have known magnitudes. Use the map, Figure 32–3, to identify the stars in the photograph and measure the diameter of each labeled star image using the wedge scale. Trace the scale shown in Figure 32–3 on tracing paper or plastic.

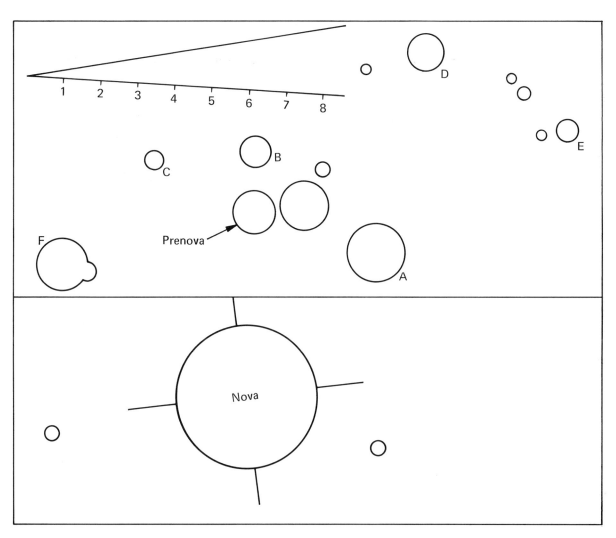

Figure 32-3. Finding chart for stars in Figure 32-2. Trace wedge scale on thin paper to measure diameters of star images in Figure 32-2.

Slide the wedge scale over the photograph until the star to be measured just fits between the lines. Record the number on the scale as the diameter of the star image. In the example in Figure 32–4 the reading is 5.6.

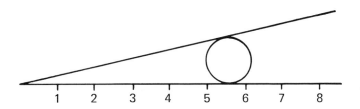

Figure 32-4. Illustration of use of wedge scale to measure diameter of star image.

activity

1. Record the numbers determined with the wedge scale in Table 32-2.

Table 32–2

Star	Diameter	m_v
A	_____	15.2
B	_____	16.4
C	_____	17.1
D	_____	16.3
E	_____	16.6
F	_____	14.5
Prenova	_____	?

2. Plot the known magnitudes versus your measurements in Figure 32-5. Do not plot star F or the prenova. Draw a smooth curve that comes as close as possible to the plotted points. Because of the errors in the data this line will probably not pass through all the points.

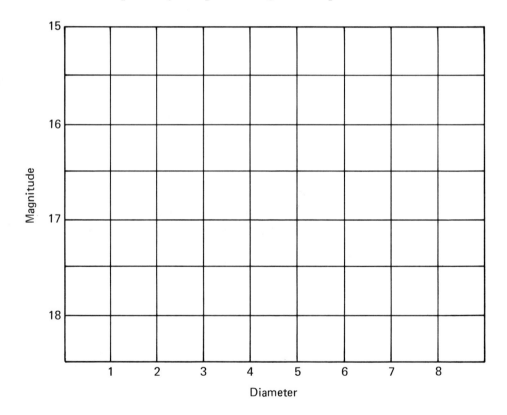

Figure 32-5. Form for the calibration curve of the data in Table 32-2.

3. Plot star F on the graph. Why should you not use it to draw the line? (*Hint*: Inspect the image).

4. You have measured the diameter of the prenova image. To what magnitude does this diameter correspond? $m_v =$ _____

   The two astronomers at Indiana University used this same process to calculate the magnitude of the prenova. Their answer was 16.1.

5. You know the magnitude of the prenova (question 4) and you know the maximum brightness of the nova (see page 212). Use your knowledge of the magnitude system to calculate the factor by which the nova increased its brightness.

6. If most novae on the average attain a maximum brightness corresponding to absolute magnitude −6, what is the distance to this nova?

supplementary material

Students may be interested in examining the original paper on which this exercise was based. M.S. Burkhead and M.A. Seeds: *The Astrophysical Journal*, **160**: L51 (1970).

exercise

33

the distance to a planetary nebula

1 materials   Millimeter rule.

2 purpose   Measuring distances in astronomy is never easy and many ingenious ways have been devised to get the distance to a star. This exercise will allow you to measure the distance to a planetary nebula using one of the most ingenious methods yet devised.

3 planetary nebulae   Planetary nebulae were so named by the early telescopic astronomers because they looked like planets through the telescope. We now know that a planetary nebula is actually a shell of gas thrown off by a star during a particular period in its life.

activity

1. Read in your text about planetary nebulae and discuss their formation.

2. Why do they sometimes look like rings?

4 **the expansion of the nebula**

Most things in the sky change very slowly, but in a few cases changes can be seen over a number of decades. Figure 33–1 contains a photograph that demonstrates that the planetary nebula NGC 6572 is expanding. It was smaller in 1916 than it was in 1961.

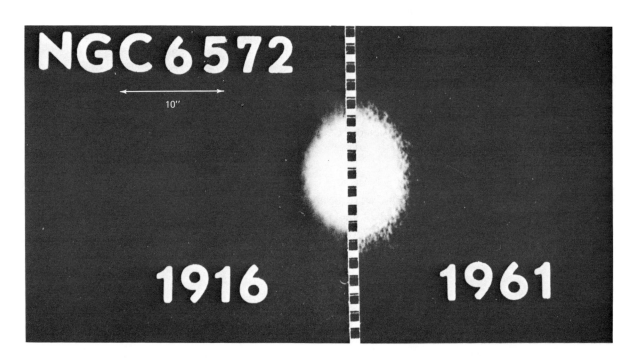

Figure 33-1. Two photographs of the planetary nebula NGC 6572 taken 45 years apart show the expansion of the nebula. [M. H. Liller, B. L. Welther, and W. Liller: *The Astrophysical Journal*, **144**(1): 280–290 (1966). Copyright by The University of Chicago 1966.]

activity

1. The arrow on the photograph is 10″ of arc long. Measure its length in millimeters. Length of arrow = _____ mm.

2. Divide this number by 10 to find the length of 1″ of arc on the photograph.

$$1″ \text{ of arc} = \underline{\hspace{3cm}} \text{ mm}$$

$$1 \text{ mm} = \underline{\hspace{3cm}} ″ \text{ of arc}$$

3. Use your millimeter rule to measure the diameter of the nebula in the 1916 photograph and in the 1961 photograph. (See Figure 33–2.) Convert your measurements to seconds of arc, and then divide by 2 to find the radius.

Diameter (1961) = \underline{\hspace{2cm}} mm = \underline{\hspace{2cm}}″ of arc

Diameter (1916) = \underline{\hspace{2cm}} mm = \underline{\hspace{2cm}}″ of arc

Radius (1961)   = \underline{\hspace{2cm}} mm = \underline{\hspace{2cm}}″ of arc

Radius (1916)   = \underline{\hspace{2cm}} mm = \underline{\hspace{2cm}}″ of arc

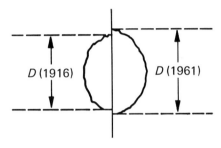

Figure 33-2. Sketch of planetary nebula shown in Figure 33-1 indicating diameters to be measured.

4. Now subtract the radius (1916) from the radius (1961) to find the change in radius, $\Delta R = \underline{\hspace{3cm}}″$ of arc

5. The nebula increased its radius by ΔR in the 45 years between 1916 and 1961. Therefore, its angular rate of expansion is

$$w = \frac{\Delta R}{45} = \underline{\hspace{3cm}}″ \text{ of arc/year}$$

In studying this nebula with a spectrograph, astronomers have found a Doppler shift in the spectrum that implies that the front of the nebula is approaching us at a velocity of 17 km/sec. This is evidently the velocity with which the nebula is expanding.

We know how fast the nebula is expanding in seconds of arc per year and in kilometers per second. That is enough data to give us the distance to the nebula.

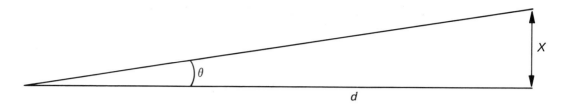

Figure 33-3. Diagram shows linear diameter X, angular diameter θ, and distance d of nebula.

5 the distance In Figure 33–3, which cannot be drawn to scale, the diameter X of an object such as the planetary nebula NGC 6572 will be very much less than its distance from us, represented by d. Therefore we may assume that we are dealing with a thin sector of a circle in which X is considered as an arc and d as the radius of a circle. In such a case the arc X divided by the radius d gives the central angle in radians (the radian is a pure number). This central angle θ is the angular diameter of the planetary nebula and is given by

$$\frac{X}{d} = \theta \text{ radians} \tag{33-1}$$

Generally the angular diameter θ is measured in seconds of arc rather than in radians, and the diameter X of the planetary nebula is given in kilometers. The quantity d will be expressed in parsecs. If 1 radian is 206,265″ of arc and 1 parsec (pc) is 3.0856×10^{13} km, then

$$\frac{X(\text{km})}{3.0856 \times 10^{13} \ (\text{km pc}^{-1}) \ d \ (\text{pc})} = \frac{\theta \ (\text{sec of arc})}{206,265 \ (\text{sec of arc}) \ \text{radian}^{-1}} \tag{33-2}$$

where θ is in seconds of arc and d is in parsecs.

Suppose instead of a distance X km, we had a velocity v km sec^{-1}. Our angular diameter θ in seconds of arc will be replaced by an angular velocity θ' (seconds of arc) sec^{-1}. Using these time rates equation (33–2) becomes

$$\frac{v \text{ km sec}^{-1}}{3.0856 \times 10^{13} \ (\text{km pc}^{-1}) \ d \ (\text{pc})} = \frac{\theta'(\text{sec of arc}) \ \text{sec}^{-1}}{206,265 \ (\text{sec of arc}) \ \text{radian}^{-1}} \tag{33-3}$$

In astronomy, angular velocity is usually expressed in seconds of arc per year. Since there are 3.156×10^7 sec in a year, we let 3.156×10^7 sec yr^{-1} θ' (sec of arc) sec^{-1} = w (sec of arc) yr^{-1} or

$$\theta' \ (\text{sec of arc}) \ \text{sec}^{-1} = \frac{w \ (\text{sec of arc}) \ \text{yr}^{-1}}{3.156 \times 10^7 \ \text{sec yr}^{-1}} \tag{33-4}$$

Substituting (33–4) into (33–3) yields

222

$$\frac{v \text{ km sec}^{-1}}{3.0856 \times 10^{13} \text{ (km pc}^{-1}) \, d \text{ (pc)}}$$

$$= \frac{w \text{ (sec of arc) yr}^{-1}}{3.156 \times 10^{7} \text{ sec yr}^{-1} \times 206{,}265 \text{ (sec of arc) radian}^{-1}} \tag{33-5}$$

Solving equation (33-5) for d, we obtain

$$d = \frac{v}{4.74\, w} \text{ pc} \tag{33-6}$$

where v is in kilometers per second and w is in seconds of arc per year.

problems

1. Use your value of the expansion, w, in seconds of arc per year and the spectroscopic velocity of expansion $v = 17$ km/sec to calculate the distance to the planetary nebula. $d = $ _____ parsecs.

2. Suppose another student does this exercise and obtains a diameter of the photographic image that is 1 mm larger than your measurement. What will he get for the distance to the nebula? $d = $ _____ parsecs.

A number of astronomers have tried to estimate the distance to this nebula in a number of ways. Table 33-1 contains their estimates. The last line has been left blank for you. Fill in your name and data. How does your result compare with the others?

Table 33-1

Author	Date	Distance(pc)
Berman	1937	300
Vorontxov-Velyaminov	1948	600
Shklovsky	1956	300
O'Dell	1962	200
Minkowski	1964	400
Seaton	1965	180

6 the age of the nebula

We now have enough data to calculate the age of the nebula. We know its distance, its angular diameter, and its rate of expansion.

The diameter of the nebula is given by

$$X = (1.50 \times 10^8)\, \theta\, d \text{ (km)}$$

which can be easily derived from equation (33–2).

problems

1. Use your value of θ which is the diameter of the nebula in seconds of arc and d the distance in parsecs to calculate the diameter X of the nebula in kilometers. Divide by 2 to find the radius R of the nebula.

$$\theta = \underline{\hspace{2cm}}'' \text{ of arc}$$

$$d = \underline{\hspace{2cm}} \text{ parsecs}$$

$$X = \underline{\hspace{2cm}} \text{ km}$$

$$R = \underline{\hspace{2cm}} \text{ km}$$

2. (a) If the nebula has been expanding at a constant rate of 17 km/sec, how many seconds has it been since it formed?

$$T = \frac{R}{17} = \underline{\hspace{2cm}} \text{ sec}$$

(b) Divide by the number of seconds in a year to find the age of the nebula in years.

$$T = \underline{\hspace{2cm}} \text{ years}$$

3. Suppose the expansion of the nebula is speeding up. (There is evidence that this is the case.) Then is your distance too large or too small? What about your estimate of the age?

Students may like to examine the original journal article on which this exercise was based. The paper is by M.H. Liller, B.L. Welther, and W. Liller, *The Astrophysical Journal*, **144** (1): 280 (1966).

A careful analysis of planetary nebulae has been written by Dr. Lawrence Aller and appeared in 14 parts in *Sky and Telescope*, **37**: 282 (May 1969) and subsequent issues.

observing Delta Cephei

1 materials   None.

2 purpose   This exercise will guide you in a continuing program of observations of the magnitude of the variable star Delta Cephei. You will observe the star on a number of evenings and obtain a light curve to determine the period and amplitude of the variation.

3 locating Delta Cephei   In September and October in the late evenings, Cepheus is located about 20° above the north celestial pole. Holding Figure 34–1 upright before you at arms length will give you the approximate orientation of the constellation (See also the star chart on page 291).

Notice that Cepheus is shaped somewhat like an inverted house, with the peaked roof pointed in the general direction of the north celestial pole. Near the upper right corner of the inverted house is the star Delta Cephei.

Locate Delta Cephei and all of the other stars shown on the map. Only the brighter stars are shown. Be certain you have located these stars correctly.

4 observations   The numbers on the map give the magnitudes of the stars with decimal point omitted. Thus 46 means 4.6 magnitude. No magnitude is given for Delta Cephei because it is a variable star and changes its brightness from night to night.

Each night at dark check the sky; if it is clear take your map outside and observe the apparent magnitude of Delta Cephei. Very carefully compare Delta Cephei with the other stars, and in each case decide whether it is brighter or fainter. For example, on some night we might decide that it is brighter than 4.2 but fainter than 3.6. Then we ask how much brighter, and finally estimate its magnitude. On some night we might conclude that it is very slightly fainter than 3.6 and much brighter than 4.2 so its estimated magnitude might be recorded as 3.7.

Each night record your estimate of the magnitude of Delta Cephei to the nearest tenth of a magnitude. Continue this process until you have enough observations to estimate the period of the star.

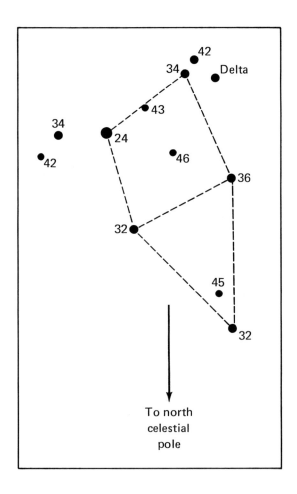

Figure 34-1. The stars in Cepheus. Numbers beside each star represent the magnitude of the star with the decimal point omitted. Thus 42 means 4.2 magnitude.

activity

Record your data in Table 34–1.

Table 34–1 Observations of Delta Cephei

Date	Time	Magnitude

5 determining the period
Plot your observations on the graph in Figure 34–2. If you observe the star on dates not included in the graph, construct your own graph. The interval between two successive maxima or minima of light variation is the period of the star.

activity

1. How do you treat nights when the sky is cloudy?

2. What is the amplitude of the variation?

observing delta cephei

3. Is the variation shaped like a sine curve or is it distorted?

4. Write a summary of everything you can conclude about the variation of this star.

5. In your textbook, look up "Cepheid variables" and summarize what is known about them. Is there a relation between the period of a Cepheid variable and its luminosity? Why are they important?

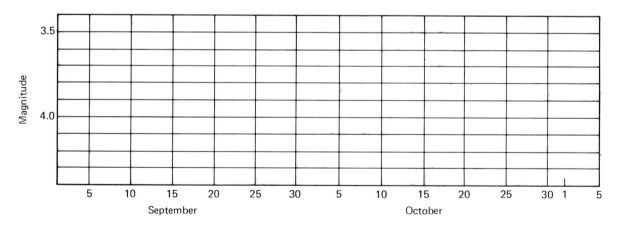

Figure 34-2. Graph for the light curve of Delta Cephei.

6 Julian day determination

If you have accumulated many observations you may wish to combine them to form a single light curve by calculating the **Julian date (J.D.)** of each observation. The J.D. is the number of days that have elapsed since 12:00 noon January 1, 4713 B.C.

For a given date we look up the J.D. in the table of "Universal and Sidereal Times" to be found in *The American Ephemeris and Nautical Almanac* for the current year. We take the J.D. number corresponding to the Greenwich date, not necessarily the date on which we have made the observation. Consider the following example:

Example. An observation of Delta Cephei was made at zone time (Z.T.) $22^h 35^m$ in longitude $76°\ 20'$W, [zone description (Z.D.) 5^h] on December 14, 1975. Find the J.D.

Solution

Z.T.	$22^h 35^m$	Dec. 14, 1975
Z.D.	5^h	
G.M.T. = U.T.	$3^h 35^m$	Dec. 15, 1975
J.D.	2442761.5000	for 0^h G.M.T. Dec. 15, 1975
Correction	.1493	($3^h 35^m = 3.5833^h = .1493^d$)
J.D.	2442761.6493	

7 phase

In order to combine our data into a single light curve, we must calculate the phase of the star's variation for each observation. To do this subtract the J.D. of the first observation, $J.D_0$, from the J.D. of each succeeding observation. We define $\Delta J.D. = J.D. - J.D_0$.

From many past observations of Delta Cephei we know that its period $P = 5.36634$ days. $\Delta J.D.$ divided by P gives the number of cycles through which the variation has gone since the first observation in the series. Since we do not care about the whole number of cycles, we drop all digits to the left of the decimal point and record the remaining decimal fraction as the phase of the observation.

Example. Suppose the first observation in our series of observations was made on $J.D_0 = 2442721.6537$. Our observation at Z.T. $22^h 35^m$ on December 14, 1975 was made on $J.D. = 2442761.6493$.

$$\Delta J.D. = J.D. - J.D_0 = 39.9956^d$$

$$\frac{\Delta J.D.}{P} = \frac{39.9956}{5.36634} = 7.4530 \text{ cycles}$$

The phase is .4530 cycle.

activity

1. Complete Table 34–2 for your observations of Delta Cephei.

Table 34-2

J.D.	ΔJ.D. = J.D. $-$ J.D.$_0$	Phase	Magnitude

2. Plot all your data from Table 34–2 in Figure 34–3.

    (a) What is the amplitude of the star's variation? _____

    (b) Is the light curve sinusoidal? _____

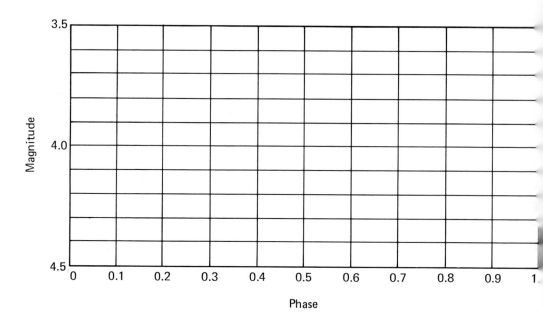

Figure 34-3. Graph for Delta Cephei light curve reduced to a single cycle.

exercise

35

the stars in Orion

1 materials   None.

2 purpose   The sky is not eternal, not fixed. It is continuously changing as the stars change, grow old, die, as new stars are born, and as the stars move across the sky. This exercise will demonstrate how a familiar constellation is changing.

3 proper motions   The angular change in position of a star per year across the sky is called its proper motion and is represented by the symbol μ. Proper motion is measured in seconds of arc per year and is determined by measuring the position of the star on two dates separated by many years.

Just as we might measure the motion of a ship at sea by the number of miles it travels north or south per day and the number of miles it travels east or west per day, we measure the motion of a star by the distance in seconds of arc it travels north or south per year and the distance in seconds of arc it travels east or west per year. The north-south motion represents a change in declination, and this component of μ is called the proper motion in declination, μ_δ. The component of μ in the east-west direction is called the proper motion in right ascension, μ_a. If the star moves northward, μ_δ is positive. If it travels eastward, μ_a is positive. If it travels in the other directions then the corresponding proper motions are negative.

The proper motions of most bright stars are much less than $1''$ of arc per year. This is a very small angle. A sheet of paper viewed edge on at arms length is about $30''$ of arc thick. It would take most stars 30 to 3000 years to move that far across the sky.

233

Table 35-1 The Stars in Orion

Star	R.A.	Dec.	μ_a	μ_δ	Spectral Type
Alpha	5^h 54^m	$+7°$ $24'$	0.027	0.007	
Beta	5 13	-8 14	0.001	0.000	
Gamma	5 24	$+6$ 19	-0.006	-0.014	
Delta	5 30	-0 19	0.001	-0.001	
Epsilon	5 35	-1 13	0.000	0.000	
Zeta	5 39	-1 57	0.004	-0.002	
Kappa	5 46	-9 41	0.004	-0.002	
Iota	5 34	-5 56	0.003	0.004	
Theta	5 34	-5 25	0.003	0.003	

In Table 35-1 only the components of the proper motion are given because the total proper motion μ may be determined from the components, μ_a and μ_δ. See Figure 35-1.

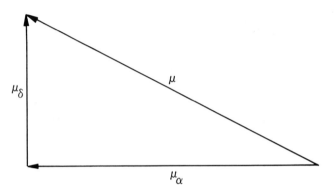

Figure 35-1. The relation between the proper motion in right ascension μ_a and declination μ_δ, and the total proper motion μ of a star near the celestial equator.

4 Orion

Plot in Figure 35-2 the positions of the stars in Orion by consulting the right ascensions and declinations listed in Table 35-1. The result will be a star chart showing the constellation Orion as it appears in our sky. Compare this with the star chart on page 289.

Trace the scale shown in Figure 35-2 and use it to draw in lightly arrows representing μ_a and μ_δ for each star as shown in Figure 35-1. Since μ_a and μ_δ are so small, plot the distance the star would travel in 1,000,000 years instead of in 1 year. Thus, Alpha Orionis has a μ_a of 0.027″ of arc per year. In 1,000,000 years it will travel 27,000″ of arc. Since μ_a is positive we conclude that the star is traveling eastward (to the left) in the constellation.

Now draw in the hypotenuse of the triangle for each star, showing its total motion across the sky for a period of 1,000,000 years.

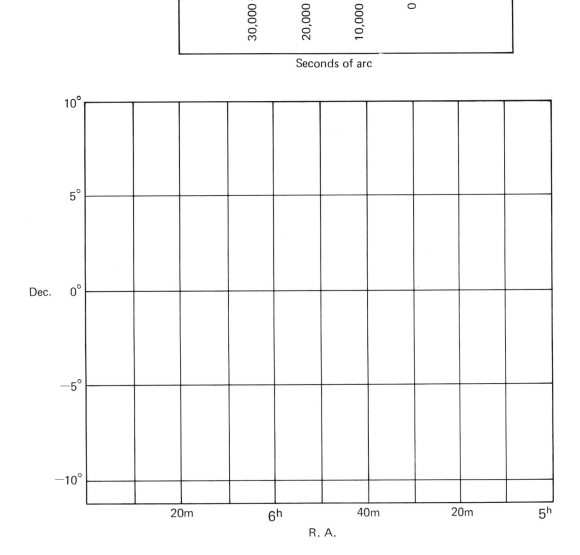

Figure 35-2. Area of sky near Orion. Plot star positions according to right ascension and declination. Scale for measurement of proper motion is in seconds of arc.

Orion in 1,000,000 years.

Place a blank piece of paper over your diagram and draw dots or stars at the tip of each arrow, μ, to show where the star will be 1,000,000 years from now. Would Orion be recognizable?

Orion 1,000,000 years ago.

Extend the arrows you have drawn backwards to show where these stars were 1,000,000 years ago. Again use a blank piece of paper to make a map of Orion as it appeared then. Man has been on earth for at least 1,500,000 years, so early man would have seen quite a different constellation pattern from the Orion we know.

5 assumptions   We have made some assumptions in making these maps. We have assumed that the stars are moving in straight lines. We know that each of these stars is moving in a curved orbit about the center of our galaxy, but in just 1,000,000 years they will not have moved very far along in their orbits and the curve in their paths should not be apparent. In the life of the galaxy, 1,000,000 years is not a very long time.

We have also assumed that the proper motions in Table 35–1 are correct. However, these quantities are very difficult to measure and there are probably some small errors in the values listed. Suppose the components of the proper motion of Alpha Orionis given in the table are too small by 0.001″ of arc per year. Increase the table values for this star by 0.001 and replot the motion of the star. How much of a difference will this small error make in the position of the star 1,000,000 years from now?

optional exercise

We have also assumed that these stars will still be bright stars in 1,000,000 years, and that they were bright stars 1,000,000 years ago. Look up the spectral types of these stars and estimate their ages and life expectancies. Consult your *Observer's Handbook* for spectral types and your text book to estimate life expectancies. Now write a paragraph or two describing how the brightness and the color of the stars in Orion might change in the future and how they might have looked in the past.

the motion of stars

1 materials   None.

2 purpose   This exercise will demonstrate how we can use the very slow motions of the stars to gain information about the universe. In this exercise we will deduce the distance to a group of stars in two ways and see how the stars in the cluster are moving.

3 proper motions   The angular change in the position of a star per year across the sky is called its **proper motion** and is represented by the symbol, μ. Proper motion is measured in seconds of arc per year and is determined by measuring the position of the star on two dates separated by many years.

   The proper motion of a star is usually expressed as two components. Its east-west motion is called μ_a, the proper motion in right ascension. If the star is moving eastward across the sky then its right ascension is increasing and μ_a is positive. The north-south motion of the star is the proper motion in declination. If the star is moving northward on the sky then its declination is increasing and μ_δ is positive.

4 the motions of a group of stars   The data in Table 36–1 gives the positions and proper motions of most of the stars brighter than 6.5 magnitude in the part of the sky between $4^h\ 14^m$ and $4^h\ 22^m$ of right ascension and between $+45°$ and $-45°$ of declination. The data given are right ascension a, declination δ, μ_a, μ_δ, spectral type, v_r the radial velocity, p the parallax, and V the apparent visual magnitude.

Table 36-1 Positions and Motions of Stars

a	δ	μ_a	μ_δ	Spectral Type	v_r	p	V
$4^h\ 14^m$	$+13°\ 48'$	+0.117	−0.020	A9	+42		5.59
14	−23 13	+0.046	+0.032	A	− 1		6.06
15	18 30	+0.111	−0.044	dF2	+42		6.11
15	14 51	+0.110	−0.023	sgA8	+36		5.26
15	13 38	+0.114	−0.024	dF2	+37		6.17
15	−34 09	+0.010	−0.002	A2		0.007	6.36
15	5 54	−0.016	−0.048	gG6	+ 7		5.71
15	8 59	+0.055	+0.042	A3			6.54
16	− 6 29	+0.103	−0.040	G5			6.33
16	− 7 50	+0.003	−0.004	B5III			5.84
16	−44 30	+0.056	−0.046	K0	+24	−0.002	5.33
16	− 0 20	−0.015	−0.120	K2		0.005	6.08
16	−20 53	+0.028	−0.007	A2V	+32	0.001	5.31
16	13 50	+0.114	−0.025	Am	+41		5.71
16	25 24	+0.020	−0.022	B9.5V	+20		5.38
16	20 35	+0.004	+0.000	gM0	− 9	0.012	6.04
17	42 12	+0.028	−0.032	B9		0.002	5.96
17	17 18	+0.110	−0.031	K0III	+38	0.016	3.76
17	−25 58	+0.045	−0.049	dF2	+17	0.049	5.95
18	20 45	+0.020	−0.029	B9V	+35		5.89
18	16 33	+0.107	−0.029	Am			5.64
18	33 54	+0.025	−0.045	B7V	+13		5.54
18	24 04	+0.010	−0.010	B3V	−32		6.14
18	33 44	+0.047	−0.073	dF5		0.003	5.73
18	17 13	+0.113	−0.039	A7V	+38	0.016	4.80
18	9 14	−0.015	−0.006	A2	− 4	−0.005	5.12
19	− 3 59	−0.049	−0.057	A2V	−11	0.007	5.17
19	−25 07	+0.016	−0.017	K5			5.82
19	18 49	+0.108	−0.045	A9n	+37		5.97
19	−35 47	−0.011	+0.001	G5			6.38
19	22 04	+0.100	−0.048	A7V	+40		4.22
19	21 58	+0.113	−0.054	A5n	+32		5.28
20	17 42	+0.112	−0.029	A2IV	+35	0.019	4.30
20	31 13	+0.077	−0.118	K1III	+28		5.18
20	15 43	+0.109	−0.029	dF5	+36	0.041	6.46
20	22 35	+0.108	−0.047	F0III–IV	+35	0.033	4.29
20	−34 15	+0.056	+0.052	M1III	+24	−0.014	3.96
21	15 23	+0.115	−0.023	F0V	+41	0.003	4.48
21	14 29	+0.000	−0.033	G8III	+32	0.013	4.81
21	8 22	+0.003	−0.014	B5	+14		6.06
21	−34 59	−0.020	−0.106	F5			6.54
21	22 46	+0.010	−0.017	B6V	+ 5		5.37
22	1 52	+0.066	−0.044	K1III	+21		6.24

Plot the proper motion components μ_a and μ_δ of each of these stars on the diagram in Figure 36-1. Note that the position of a star on this diagram

stars

indicates something about how it is moving on the sky. Stars moving to the north are in the upper half of the diagram, those moving to the east are in the right half of the diagram.

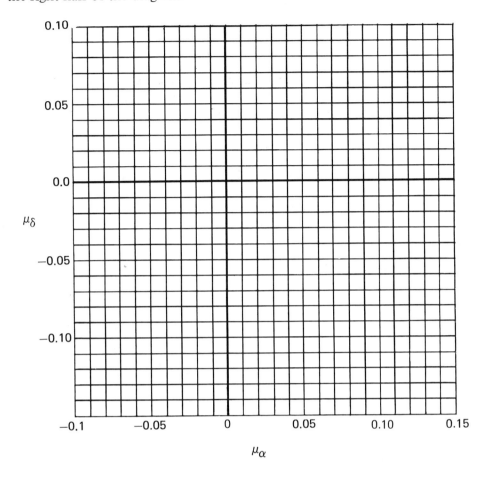

Figure 36-1. Proper motion diagram. Plot stars according to proper motion in right ascension μ_α and declination μ_δ.

activity

When you have finished your diagram locate a cluster of about 16 points on the right side of the graph. The fact that these stars all have about the same location in the diagram means they are all moving in the same general direction. Estimate from the graph the average motion of this group.

Average μ_a = _____   Average μ_δ = _____

5 identification

Examine Table 36–1 and make a mark beside each star that is in the group. These stars seem to be related in some way.

activity

1. Estimate their right ascensions and declinations and plot their average position on one of the star charts following the appendices. What is this group of stars called?

    Average R.A. = _____   Average Dec. = _____ .

    Name of cluster _____

2. The group of stars you have discovered is called a galactic cluster of stars. All of the stars seem to have formed at about the same time from the same cloud of gas and dust. From Table 36–1 estimate the average parallax and average radial velocity for these stars.

    Average p = ——————   Average v_r = _____

3. How can we be sure a star is a member of the cluster? For example if a star has $\mu_a = 0.110$ and $\mu_\delta = -0.023$ and $v_r = +44$ km/sec, would you classify it a member of the cluster or not? Explain your answer.

4. The brightest star in this area of the sky is Aldebaran. The data for Aldebaran are $\mu_a = 0.069$, $\mu_\delta = -0.190$, $p = 0.048$, $v_r = +54$, V = 0.86 and it is a K5III star.

    (a) Is Aldebaran a member of the cluster? _____

(b) How might the spectral type be a help in making this decision?

6   distance to the cluster

Not all of the stars in this cluster have had their parallaxes determined. For those that have parallaxes in Table 36–1, find the average parallax of the cluster and the distance to the cluster.

Average parallax = _____   Distance to cluster = _____pc

This is not a very good method for determining the distance to the cluster because only a few stars in the cluster have known parallaxes and because the parallaxes in this case cannot be measured very accurately.

Of the stars we have identified in the cluster, some are giants and some are main sequence stars. The spectral types of the main sequence stars are followed by a Roman numeral V or preceded by a "d" in Table 36–1. If all of these stars were at a distance of 10 pc, their apparent magnitudes would equal their absolute magnitudes. They are not necessarily at 10 pc, but they are all at about the same distance from the Earth. Consequently their apparent magnitudes differ from their absolute magnitudes by some constant called the distance modulus. If we find the distance modulus we can find the distance.

Figure 36–2 is an H-R diagram with smooth curves showing the location of the main sequence, giants, and supergiants. Although we do not know the absolute magnitudes of the stars in the cluster, we can plot them on this diagram as if their apparent magnitudes were absolute magnitudes. Plot the main sequence stars as dots and the giants as crosses.

activity

1. Since all the stars are at the same distance from us we will find that they are all located above or below the H-R diagram main sequence by some constant amount. If the cluster were 10 pc away, the main sequence stars

in the cluster should fall on the smooth curve representing main sequence stars. Is the cluster closer or further away than 10 pc? _____

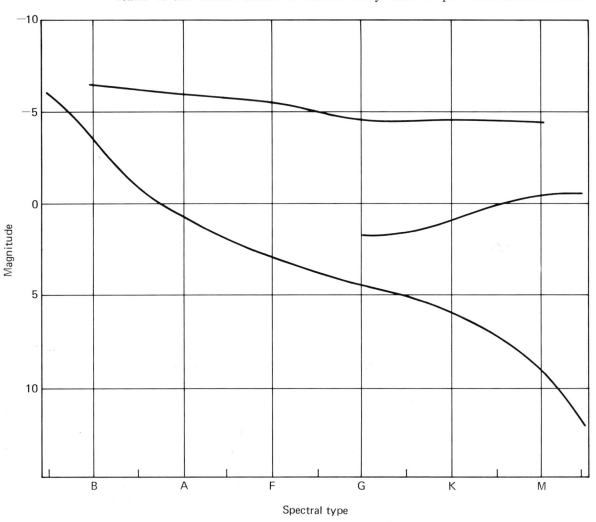

Figure 36-2. H-R diagram for use in determination of distance to star cluster.

2. For each main sequence cluster star in Figure 36–2 measure in magnitudes the distance it falls below the main sequence. Average these to find the average number of magnitudes the cluster is fainter than it would appear at a distance of 10 pc. This is called the distance modulus and is the difference between the apparent magnitude and the absolute magnitude, $m - M$. Calculate the parallax and distance using equation (36–1).

$$m - M = -5 - 5 \log p \qquad (36\text{--}1)$$

$$p = \underline{\hspace{2cm}} \qquad d = \underline{\hspace{2cm}}$$

3. Explain carefully why your two distances do not agree. How would inter-stellar absorption affect your results? Is there any reason why the average parallax might be too large?

4. Average your two values for the distance and compare it with the distance given in your text book or *Observers Handbook.*

Average distance = _____

Distance (*Observers Handbook*) = _____

optional activity

Read about the moving cluster method for determining the distance to this cluster and describe it in a few paragraphs.

unit V

galaxies and cosmology

the spiral arms near the Sun

1 materials

None.

2 purpose

This exercise will allow you to study the structure of our galaxy and to examine the spiral arms near the Sun.

3 galactic coordinates

Stars can be located in the sky by their right ascension and declination. This is a convenient system, but it has nothing to do with the distribution of stars in our galaxy. If we are to study our galaxy we need a set of galactic coordinates.

The galactic equator is defined as the circle on the sky that follows the center of the path of stars we call the Milky Way. This hazy strip of light is, in fact, the disc of our galaxy, and the galactic equator represents the plane of that disc. Galactic latitude, b, is measured in degrees above or below the celestial equator. A star on the galactic equator has $b - 0°$. A star above the galactic equator would have a positive b and a star below the galactic equator would have a negative b. Galactic longitude, l, is measured along the galactic equator starting from the direction toward the galactic center and ranges from 0° to 360°.

By giving the galactic latitude and longitude of a star, we give its direction in the galaxy. If l and b are both zero for a star, then the star is located in the direction toward the center of the galaxy. If $b = 0°$ and $l = 180°$, then the star is located in the plane of the galaxy but in a direction directly away from the center.

Table 37–1 Groups of O Stars

Longitude (degrees)	Latitude (degrees)	Distance (kpc)
1	−2	3.0
7	−3	1.3
8	−2	1.4
13	−2	2.3
14	−1	1.7
18	−1	2.3
19	0	2.0
61	−1	1.8
73	1	2.3
77	0	1.5
78	0	2.0
81	0	1.5
84	−8	1.0
98	−18	0.5
99	5	0.7
104	−2	3.6
110	3	1.0
116	0	2.5
120	0	2.2
124	2	2.5
135	−3	2.3
137	2	2.1
147	1	0.9
161	−15	0.4
174	0	1.2
174	0	3.8
190	3	1.5
207	−18	0.5
209	0	1.4
286	0	3.3
288	0	1.9
295	−1	2.8
305	5	2.2
344	0	1.4
351	17	0.2

4 **the distribu-** Table 37–1 gives the galactic longitude and latitude of a number of groups of
tion of stars stars of spectral type O.   Plot the positions of these stars on Figure 37–1.

galaxies and cosmology

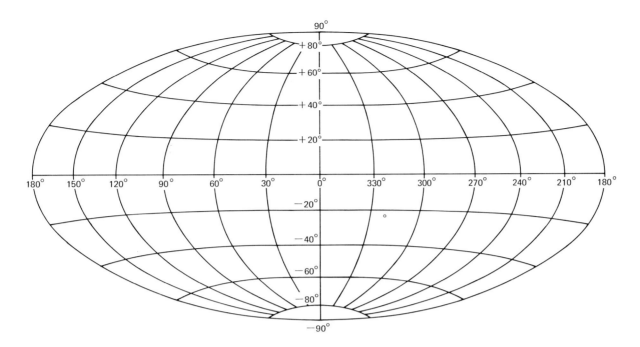

Figure 37-1. Equal area projection of celestial sphere. Horizontal scale is galactic longitude. Vertical scale is galactic latitude.

Now examine Table 37–2. These stars are all long-period variables, and are cool giant stars. Use a red pencil or else make small crosses to plot these stars on Figure 37–1.

activity

Why do we find groups of young stars only near the galactic equator but older giant stars scattered all over the sky? *Hint*: Perhaps you will need to read about stellar populations in order to answer this question.

Table 37-2 Long Period Variable Giant Stars

Longitude (degrees)	Latitude (degrees)
113	−13
310	−10
56	− 9
158	−37
21	60
144	19
107	71
215	11
282	− 3
298	13
77	−80
322	0
326	81
61	52
269	37
91	− 5
272	−39
60	−26
124	−55
355	−62
74	48
259	38

5 stars in the spiral arms

Figure 37–2 is a sketch of what our galaxy might look like. The spiral arms are shown wrapped around the nucleus at the center. From the position of the Sun it is not possible to see stars in all of the spiral arms because of the interstellar dust that obscures the distant stars. But bright stars can be seen in the nearer spiral arms. Figure 37–3 represents that part of the galaxy within a few kiloparsecs of the Sun.

Plot the stars in Table 37–1 on Figure 37–3 using galactic longitudes and distances in kiloparsecs. Notice that these groups of young stars are all located in spiral arms. In fact we could use these kinds of objects to trace the spiral pattern. Such objects associated with spiral arms are called spiral tracers.

galaxies and cosmology

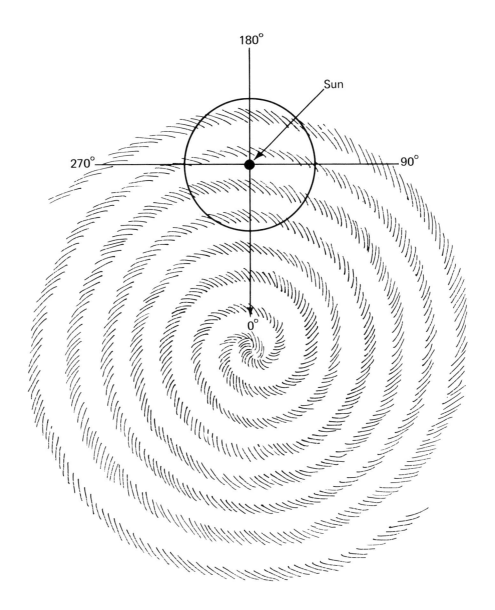

Figure 37-2. Idealized view of our galaxy. Axes indicate galactic longitude. The circle about the Sun has a radius of 3.5 kpc. Compare with Figure 37-3.

questions

1. (a) Why are these localized groups of hot young stars spiral tracers?

(b) Why are they located only in the spiral arms?

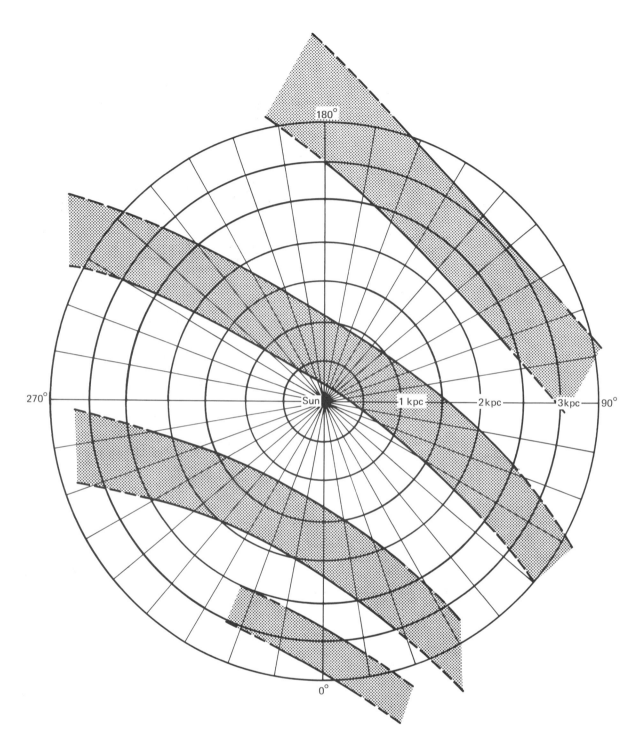

Figure 37-3. The plane of the galaxy near the Sun. Plot data using distance in kiloparsecs and galactic longitude. Compare with Figure 37-2.

galaxies and cosmology

6 spiral arms   Figure 37–3 represents only a small part of our galaxy. Draw an arrow on the figure to point from the Sun toward the center of the galaxy.

question

How far is it from the Sun to the center of the galaxy?

The rotation of the galaxy is clockwise about the center (see Figure 37–2). Thus all of the stars in our Figure 37–3 are moving in their orbits toward the right. Draw an arrow to show the direction of rotation of the galaxy.

Notice that the spiral arms are not perpendicular to the line drawn to the center of the galaxy. The arms are tilted slightly and seem to be trailing as the galaxy rotates. Notice also that the Sun is not in a spiral arm but is on the inside edge of the arm. This arm is called the Carina-Cygnus arm. The next arm inward from the Carina-Cygnus arm is the Sagittarius arm, and the arm outward from the Carina-Cygnus arm is the Perseus arm. These names refer to the constellations located in these directions. Label these arms in Figure 37–3.

The spiral arms are not smooth. There are many knots, spurs, and branches scattered along the arms. Located on the outer edge of the Carina-Cygnus arm in longitude 180° to 210° is a bulge or spur of stars, gas, and dust known as the Orion spur. A few of the groups of stars we have plotted in Figure 37–3 are members of the Orion spur.

activity

1. Consult your textbook and try to locate a photograph of a spiral galaxy such as M51, The Whirlpool Galaxy. Try to find such a bulge as the Orion spur in the photograph.

2. If the photograph were of our own galaxy, where would the Sun be located? _____

3. Can you decide which way the galaxy in the photograph is rotating? How?

exercise
38

the expansion
of the universe

1 materials   Millimeter rule.

2 purpose   By measuring the Doppler shift of absorption lines in the spectra of galaxies, their velocities of recession may be determined and the expansion of the universe shown. Both classical and relativistic Doppler formulas are examined and the velocity-distance relation is introduced. The age of the universe is calculated from Hubble's constant.

3 measurement of red shifts   Examine Figure 38–1, which shows the spectra of five galaxies. Each spectrum is bounded above and below by a bright line comparison spectrum. Notice that the calcium II lines, H and K, do not appear where they should in each spectrum. In fact they are shifted toward the red, and the further away the galaxy is the further the lines are shifted.

One explanation of this is that the galaxies are moving away from us, the universe is expanding, and the spectral lines are shifted by the Doppler effect toward the red end of the spectrum. If that is the case, we can calculate the radial velocity v_r of each galaxy by measuring the amount by which the wavelengths are changed. The radial velocity is given by the classical Doppler formula

$$v_r = c\, \frac{\Delta\lambda}{\lambda} \qquad\qquad (38\text{–}1)$$

where c is the speed of light, 3×10^5 km sec^{-1}, λ is the laboratory wavelength of a spectral line in angstrom units, and $\Delta\lambda$ is the shift of the spectral line in angstrom units.

RELATION BETWEEN RED-SHIFT AND DISTANCE
FOR EXTRAGALACTIC NEBULAE

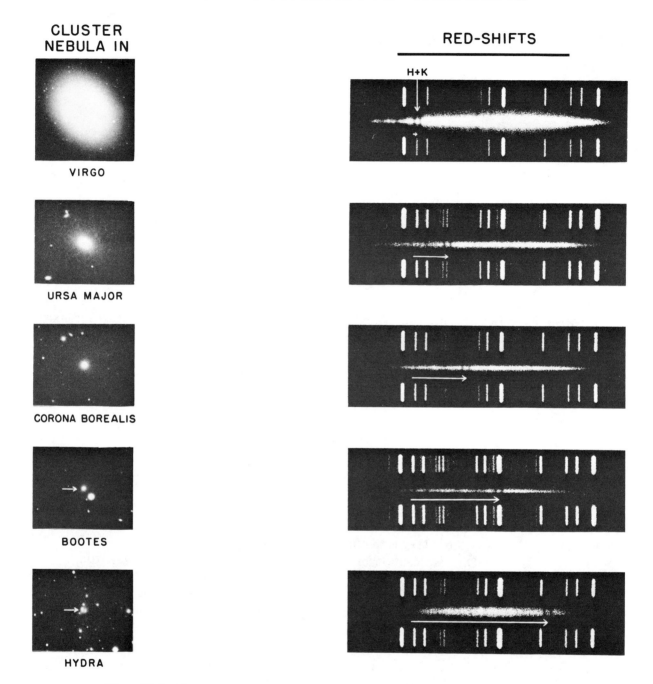

Figure 38-1. Photographs and spectra of extragalactic nebulae. The white arrow under each spectrum indicates the red shift of the H and K lines of calcium. [Courtesy Hale Observatories.]

galaxies and cosmology

1. In Figure 38–1 a white arrow has been added to each spectrum to show us how far the lines have been shifted from their normal position. Let ΔR represent the amount of shift. To the nearest tenth of a millimeter, measure this shift and record your measurements in Table 38–1 under ΔR.

Table 38–1 Red Shift Data

Galaxy Cluster	ΔR	$\Delta\lambda$	v_r	r(Mpc)
Virgo				24
Ursa Major				310
Cor. Borealis				430
Bootes				770
Hydra				1200

2. Measure to the nearest tenth of a millimeter the length of the line directly under the word "Red-shifts" in Figure 38–1. This line has been drawn to represent a distance of 1000 Å on the spectra. Record the length L of this line in millimeters. $L = $ _____mm.

3. The scale S of the spectra is given by

$$S = \frac{1000\ \text{Å}}{L\ \text{mm}} = \underline{\hspace{2cm}} \text{Å mm}^{-1}.$$

4. Multiply ΔR by the scale to obtain $\Delta\lambda$ in angstroms. If the laboratory wavelength is known, the radial velocity can be calculated. The wavelengths of the two calcium lines are 3933.67 Å and 3968.47 Å. In this exercise we will use their average wavelength, 3951 Å, to calculate the radial velocities of the galaxies in kilometers per second. Record your results in Table 38–1 under v_r.

4 **the velocity-distance relation**   In Figure 38–2, plot each galaxy's velocity versus its distance in megaparsecs (Mpc). Note that there seems to be a linear relation, but it is probably not possible to draw a straight line that passes through every one of the points.

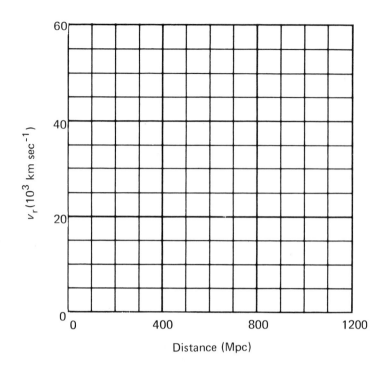

Figure 38-2. Velocity-distance diagram.

activity

1. Draw a straight line through the origin such that the points are as close to the line as possible. Why should this line pass through the origin?

2. The slope of the line you have drawn is the increase in the velocity divided by the increase in distance.

   (a) If the distance increases by 400 Mpc, the velocity will increase by _____ km sec^{-1}.

   (b) The slope is then _____ km sec^{-1} Mpc^{-1}.

   Note: This is Hubble's constant and is approximately 50 km sec^{-1} Mpc^{-1}.

galaxies and cosmology

1. We have discovered a cluster of galaxies in which the H and K lines of cal-cium are shifted by 430 Å.

    (a) What is your estimate of the distance to this cluster? _____

    (b) Upon what assumptions does your estimate depend?

2. In the quasi–stellar object PHL 1127 the Lyman alpha line of hydrogen, which should be at 1216 Å, is detected near 3648 Å.

    (a) Calculate the radial velocity of this object using the classical Doppler formula, equation (38–1).

$$v_r = \underline{\hspace{2cm}} \text{ km sec}^{-1}$$

    (b) Is this reasonable? Why?

    (c) Calculate the velocity using the relativistic equation

$$\frac{v_r}{c} = \frac{(1 + Z)^2 - 1}{(1 + Z)^2 + 1}$$

    where $Z = \frac{\Delta \lambda}{\lambda}$

$$v_r = \underline{\hspace{2cm}} \text{ km sec}^{-1}$$

    (d) When velocities are comparable with the speed of light, the relativis-tic form of the equation must be used. But when the velocities are low, say less than 10% of the speed of light, the simpler form may be used. Both forms must give nearly the same answer at low velocities.

Calculate the radial velocity of the galaxy in the Hydra cluster (Table 38–1) using the relativistic form of the equation.

$$v_r = \underline{\hspace{3cm}} \text{km sec}^{-1}$$

(e) Does the value from part (d) agree with the radial velocity you obtained with the simpler form?

3. Hubble's constant, H, has the units

$$\frac{\text{km}}{(\text{sec}) (10^6 \text{pc})}.$$

If the formula $v_r = Hr$ is expressed in the form $r/v_r = 1/H$ it is clear that $1/H$ represents time. The units for $1/H$ are

$$\frac{(\text{sec}) (10^6 \text{pc})}{\text{km}}$$

Now $1/H$ is the approximate age of the universe (the time since the last big bang). Calculate the age of the universe in years using

$$H = 50 \; \frac{\text{km}}{(\text{sec}) (10^6 \text{pc})}.$$

Hint: There are 3×10^7 sec in a year and 1 pc = 3×10^{13} km approximately.

Age of the universe $\underline{\hspace{3cm}}$ years

supplementary problems

1. Show that the formulas

$$\frac{v_r}{c} = \frac{(1 + Z)^2 - 1}{(1 + Z)^2 + 1}$$

and

$$\frac{\Delta\lambda}{\lambda} = \frac{1 + \dfrac{v_r}{c}}{\sqrt{1 - \left(\dfrac{v_r}{c}\right)^2}} - 1$$

are equivalent.
Note that $Z = \dfrac{\Delta\lambda}{\lambda}$.

2. Show that when v_r is very much less than c, $(v_r << c)$, the classical Doppler formula

$$\frac{\Delta\lambda}{\lambda} = \frac{v_r}{c}$$

may be derived from the relativistic formula. *Hint*: If $v_r << c$, what can you say about $\left(\dfrac{v_r}{c}\right)^2$?

3. If $\Delta\lambda/\lambda = .1$, show that the error in v_r (as compared with the relativistic value) is about 5% if you use the classical Doppler formula.

celestial sphere and coordinate systems

1 abbreviations

Z	zenith	♈	vernal equinox
Na	nadir	$P_n Z P_s$	observer's meridian (upper branch)
P_n	north celestial pole	Hor.	celestial horizon
P_s	south celestial pole	Ec.	ecliptic
N	north point of horizon	C.E.	celestial equator
S	south point of horizon	T	foot of hour circle through B
V.C.	vertical circle	R	foot of vertical circle through B
H.C.	hour circle	w	westward direction along C.E.
B	celestial body	NP_n	elevation of pole

		(arc)
L.S.T.	local sidereal time	$Mm♈$
L.H.A.	local hour angle	MmT
R.A.	right ascension	$♈T$
Dec.	declination	TB
Z_n	azimuth	NR
h	altitude	RB

Note: Latitude of the observer is numerically equal to the elevation of the pole.

2 horizon system

We refer to the imaginary surface on which the stars, planets, and other celestial objects appear as the celestial sphere. Because earth is small compared with the great size of this sphere, we represent the observer with earth as a point at the center of the sphere.

263

The point on the celestial sphere directly above the observer is the **zenith** (Z) and the point directly below is the **nadir** (Na). The great circle on the sphere midway between these two points is the **celestial horizon** (Hor.). A great circle drawn from the zenith to the nadir and passing through an object is called a **vertical circle** (V.C.) and is perpendicular to the celestial horizon.

One coordinate of the horizon system is **azimuth** (Z_n) which the astronomer measures from the north point of the horizon eastward around the celestial horizon to the point where the vertical circle through the star intersects the horizon. Azimuth ranges from $0°$ to $360°$. Starting from the horizon the angular distance measured along the vertical circle to the object represents the altitude h of the star. This is the second coordinate of the horizon system. Altitudes range from $0°$ to $90°$ for objects above the horizon; objects below the horizon have negative altitudes.

Since each person carries his own zenith and horizon around with him, azimuths and altitudes of objects will not be the same at all points on the Earth's surface. In addition these coordinates vary with time.

3 equator system

Those points where the Earth's axis of rotation intersects the celestial sphere are the north and south celestial poles, designated by P_n and P_s. The celestial equator midway between the poles may be considered as the intersection of the plane of the earth's equator with the celestial sphere. As one looks down on the celestial equator from the north celestial pole, a *clockwise* direction is defined to be a *westward* direction. A great circle drawn from pole to pole and passing through an object is called an **hour circle** (H.C.) and is perpendicular to the celestial equator.

The apparent path of the Sun in the sky, the **ecliptic**, is inclined at an angle of approximately $23\frac{1}{2}°$ with the celestial equator and intersects it at two points, the vernal equinox and the autumnal equinox. The symbol Υ on Figure A–1 denotes the vernal equinox, and its position with respect to the observer's meridian is determined by the local sidereal time (L.S.T.) which is the local hour angle (L.H.A.) of Υ.

The coordinates of an object in the equator system are right ascension and declination. The **right ascension** (R.A.) of an object is the arc measured from the vernal equinox *eastward* along the celestial equator to the foot of the hour circle passing through the star and is expressed in time units from 0^h to 24^h. Starting from the celestial equator, the angular distance measured along the hour circle to the object represents the **declination** (Dec.) of the object. Stars north of the celestial equator have north (+) declinations; those south of the celestial equator have south (−) declinations.

In Figure A–1 the upper branch of the observer's meridian is denoted by the arc $P_n Z P_s$. The **local hour angle** (L.H.A.) of an object is measured along the celestial equator from the upper branch of the observer's meridian (M) *westward* to the foot of the hour circle through the object and is measured in time units from 0^h to 24^h.

The local sidereal time (L.S.T.) is the local hour angle of the vernal equinox and in Figure A-1 is represented by the arc $Mm\Upsilon$. In general it is easy to verify that L.S.T. − R.A. ★ = L.H.A. ★ or L.S.T. + 24^h − R.A. ★ = L.H.A. ★.

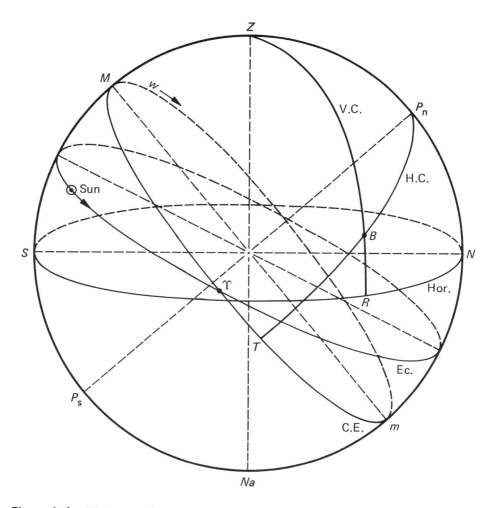

Figure A-1. Horizon and equator coordinate systems with ecliptic. Compare this with Figure 2-1 of Exercise 2, Using a Celestial Globe.

4 latitude and elevation of the pole

In Figure A-2 the polar axis and the line of sight from the observer at C to P_n may be considered to be parallel. Triangle COD is a right triangle and angle ODC is equal to angle L which is the observer's latitude. Alternate interior angles of parallel lines cut by the transversal CD are equal. This completes the demonstration that angle L is equal to angle h, that is, the latitude of the observer is numerically equal to the elevation of the pole P_n. A similar argument would hold for an observer in a southern latitude.

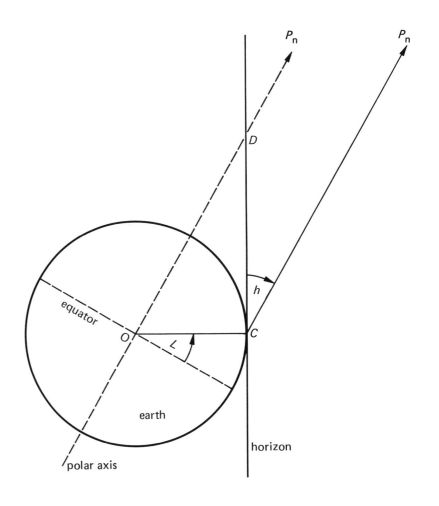

Figure A-2. The elevation h of the pole is numerically equal to the latitude L of the observer.

5 **local sidereal time**

For determination of local sidereal time refer to Exercise 6, Calculation of Sidereal Time, or Exercise 8, The Starfinder—Part I, page 41.

6 **azimuth and altitude**

Example. Where would you look for the variable star Mira at the Grundy Observatory (latitude 40° N, longitude $5^h \ 05^m \ 20^s$ W) on November 10, 1975, at zone time (Z.T.) $19^h \ 30^m$?

We calculate the L.S.T. and find the R.A. and Dec. of Mira in the *Observer's Handbook* or from a star chart.

L.S.T.	$22^h \ 43^m$	corresponding to Z.T. $19^h \ 30^m$ at the Grundy Observatory
R.A.	$\underline{02^h \ 18^m}$	
L.H.A.	$20^h \ 25^m$	
Dec.	$-3° \ 07'$	

If in Figure A–1 we delete the ecliptic and view both the celestial equator and the celestial horizon edgewise, we have a diagram similar to that shown in Figure A–3. The details for the construction of Figure A–3 will be found in Exercise 10, Locating Celestial Objects with a Coordinate Grid.

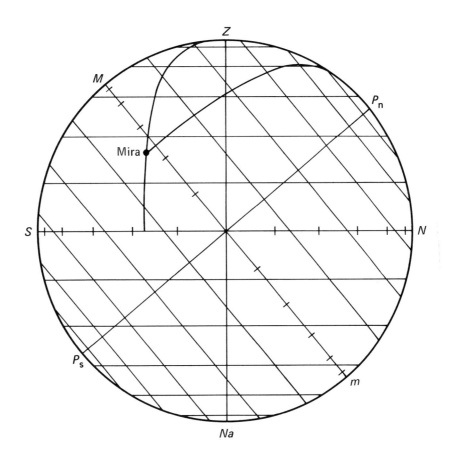

Figure A–3.   Celestial sphere showing Mira at azimuth 117° and altitude 24°.

The arc of the celestial equator that lies on the back of the sphere now coincides with the arc on the front of the sphere; likewise with the celestial horizon. In plotting the position of Mira in Figure A–3 we need to keep in mind the basic definitions and ideas illustrated in Figure A–1.

The local hour angle of Mira determines the foot of the hour circle through Mira. The hour circle arc containing Mira lies on the front of the sphere and the declination locates Mira on this arc. The vertical circle through Mira lies on the front of the sphere and we can estimate the arc from

N eastward along the celestial horizon to the foot of the vertical circle through Mira.

$$\text{Estimated azimuth:} \quad Z_n = 117°$$

$$\text{Estimated altitude:} \quad h = 24°$$

Using this information one could point to where Mira would be at the given time on the given date at the Grundy Observatory.

appendix

B

the observer's handbook

1 materials   *The Observer's Handbook* for the current year.

2 purpose   This handbook contains an ephemeris of the sun, moon, stars, planets and other celestial objects. This exercise is intended to acquaint you with the information to be found in this reference.

problems

(Reference to the index in this handbook will prove helpful.)

1. When does Easter occur this year? _____

2. From the list of "Brightest Stars" identify the stars having the following coordinates:

R.A.	Dec.	Mag. V	Scientific Name	Common Name
$00^h\ 07.3^m$	$+28°\ 58'$			
$04^h\ 34.8^m$	$+16°\ 28'$			
$07^h\ 38.2^m$	$+05°\ 17'$			
$14^h\ 49.8^m$	$-15°\ 54'$			
$16^h\ 34.6^m$	$-28°\ 10'$			

3. (a) In the table of "The Nearest Stars", what is the meaning of the symbol π? _____ Of D? _____

   (b) Which of the stars, Altair or Procyon, is closer to Earth? _____

   (c) Which is more luminous? _____

   (d) What is the apparent magnitude of the Sun? _____

   (e) Of Altair? _____ Of Barnard's star? _____

4. What is the speed of light in centimeters per second? _____

5. One astronomical unit is equivalent to _____ miles.

6. On June 21 the right ascension of the Sun is _____ and the declination of the Sun is _____.

7. What is the equatorial diameter of Jupiter? _____

8. Time by the stars is called _____ time.

9. At what local mean time does the Sun rise and set on February 12 in latitude 40° N? Rise _____, Set _____.

10. On what date in June is the Moon new? _____, Full? _____

11. On June 26 in latitude 40° N when does the Moon rise? _____ Set? _____

12. Mercury's maximum angular distance (greatest elongation) from the Sun varies between _____ and _____ degrees.

13. List the dates when Mercury may best be seen this year in the evening sky just after sunset. _____

14. Estimate the right ascension and the declination of Saturn for June 1. R.A. _____, Dec. _____

15. The _____ meteor shower will occur on or about August 12. The approximate hourly rate is _____. Is the phase of the Moon favorable for this shower? _____

16. On what date will a total eclipse of the Sun occur? _____

17. Name four lunar maria. _____, _____,

    _____, _____.

18. Name three lunar craters named after famous astronomers.

    _____, _____, _____ .

19. In what constellation is the star Sirius to be found? _____

    Castor? _____, Fomalhaut? _____, Antares? _____

20. The star RR Lyrae is a variable star. Its mean maximum magnitude is

    _____; its mean minimum magnitude is _____ .

    The period of variation of this star is _____ days.

21. The first star listed in the table of "Long Period Variable Stars" is T Cas.

    What is the meaning of 001755? _____

    _____

22. γ Leonis is a double star. It has R.A. _____ and Dec. _____ .

    The magnitude of the brighter component is _____ and the faint-

    er _____. The combined magnitude of the system is _____.

    Its distance is _____ l.y.

23. In the handbook, M42 is listed in the "Messier Catalog of Diffuse Ob-

    jects." It is in the constellation _____ , has

    R.A. _____ and Dec. _____. Under type, what is the

    meaning of DN? _____

24. An example of a globular cluster is _____ .

25. What is the nature of M57? _____

26. The Pleiades is an open cluster. It is in the constellation _____

    and has an apparent diameter of _____ minutes of arc.

27. Give the Messier designation of the following: Ring nebula _____ ,

    Orion nebula _____, Dumb-bell nebula _____, Crab ne-

    bula _____.

28. The first pulsar discovered is designated _____ and has period _____.

29. The nearest and strongest quasar is designated _____.

30. The external galaxy M31 has R.A. _____ and Dec. _____. Its distance is _____.

31. The mass of our galaxy is approximately _____ solar masses.

common logarithms

1 materials

None.

2 purpose

Whether or not a calculator is available for numerical solutions to problems, the basic concepts of logarithms need to be understood because they relate to problems of apparent and absolute magnitude and the determination of stellar distances. A brief logarithm table is appended, important properties of logarithms are listed, and a short set of exercises introduces the student to simple calculations with common logarithms.

3 definition of logarithm

The logarithm of a positive number N is the exponent x to which 10 must be raised to produce the number N, that is, if

$$\log N = x$$

then

$$10^x = N,$$

and conversely.

Examples

(a) The logarithm of 100 is 2 because $10^2 = 100$

(b) The logarithm of 200 is 2.301 because $10^{2.301} = 200$ (nearly).

Every number can be expressed as a number between 1 and 10, times a suitable power of 10. The table that follows illustrates this statement.

$320 = 3.2 \times 10^2$	$\log\ 320 = 2.505$	$10^{2.505} = 320$
$32 = 3.2 \times 10^1$	$\log\ \ 32 = 1.505$	$10^{1.505} = 32$
$3.2 = 3.2 \times 10^0$	$\log\ \ 3.2 = 0.505$	$10^{0.505} = 3.2$
$.32 = 3.2 \times 10^{-1}$	$\log\ .32 = 9.505 - 10$	$10^{-.495} = .32$
$.032 = 3.2 \times 10^{-2}$	$*\log .032 = 8.505 - 10$	
	$= -2 + .505$	
	$= -1.495$	$10^{-1.495} = .032$

*For some calculations we may prefer to use the first form, $8.505 - 10$.

Consider $\log\ 320 = 2.505$. The characteristic of the logarithm is 2, which is the digit preceding the decimal point in 2.505. The mantissa of the logarithm is .505, the digits following the decimal point in 2.505. The characteristic is obtained by inspection; the mantissa may be taken from the logarithm table.

$\log 320 = 2.505$ is reasonable since $10^2 = 100$ and $10^3 = 1000$.

And because 320 is between 100 and 1000, we would expect the logarithm of 320 to lie somewhere between 2 and 3.

4 properties of logarithms

1. The logarithm of the product of two numbers is equal to the sum of logarithms of the numbers, that is

$$\log (MN) = \log M + \log N$$

Example

$$\log 200 = \log [(2)\,(100)] = \log 2 + \log 100$$
$$= .301 + 2 = 2.301$$

2. The logarithm of the quotient of two numbers is equal to the logarithm of the numerator minus the logarithm of the denominator, that is

$$\log \frac{M}{N} = \log M - \log N$$

Example. $\log 5 = \log 10/2 = \log 10 - \log 2 = 1 - .301 = .699$

3. The logarithm of a number raised to a power is equal to the power times the logarithm of the number, that is

$$\log M^p = p \log M$$

Example. $\log 32 = \log 2^5 = 5 \log 2 = 5\,(.301) = 1.505$

5 **using a logarithm table**

A three place logarithm table follows.

	0	1	2	3	4	5	6	7	8	9
10	.000	.041	.079	.114	.146	.176	.204	.230	.255	.279
20	.301	.322	.342	.362	.380	.398	.415	.431	.447	.462
30	.477	.491	.505	.519	.531	.544	.556	.568	.580	.591
40	.602	.613	.623	.633	.643	.653	.663	.672	.681	.690
50	.699	.708	.716	.724	.732	.740	.748	.756	.763	.771
60	.778	.785	.792	.799	.806	.813	.820	.826	.833	.839
70	.845	.851	.857	.863	.869	.875	.881	.886	.892	.898
80	.903	.908	.914	.919	.924	.929	.934	.940	.944	.949
90	.954	.959	.964	.968	.973	.978	.982	.987	.991	.996

Note: Many tables omit the decimal point.

Examples

1. $\log 1 = 0$
2. $\log 10 = 1$
3. $\log 43 = 1.633$
4. $\log 2.512 = .400$
5. $\log N = 3.820$
   $N = 6600$
6. Evaluate $(2.512)^{2.9}$

   Let $N = (2.512)^{2.9}$
   $\log N = 2.9 \log 2.512$
   $\quad = 2.9\,(.400) = 1.160$
   $N = 14.5$

7. Evaluate $N = (.041)^3$

   $\log N = 3 \log (.041) = 3(8.613 - 10)$
   $\quad = 25.839 - 30$
   $\quad = 5.839 - 10$
   $N = .000069$

common logarithms

problems

1. log 6000 = _____

2. log N = 2.869

   N = _____

3. log 10^5 = _____

5. $N = (.0052)^3$

   log N = _____

   N = _____

4. log N = 8.895 − 10

   N = _____

6. $x = (2.512)^7$

   log x = _____

   x = _____

7. $x = \sqrt{56.5} = (56.5)^{1/2}$

   log x = _____

   x = _____

8. $(2.512)^{3-x} = 16$

   x = _____

9. $N = \dfrac{(45.1)\,(.0467)}{235}$

   log N = _____

   N = _____

10. (a) In the formula $M = m + 5 - 5 \log D$, if $M = -5$ and $m = 10$, then

    log D = _____ and D = _____,

    (b) If $M = -6$ and $m = 7$, then log D = _____ and

    D = _____.

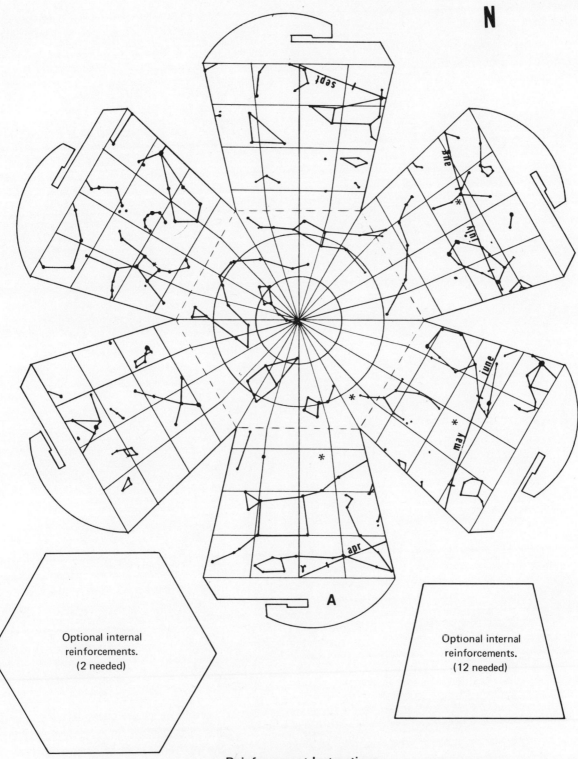

Reinforcement Instructions

After cutting and folding the two hemispheres of the pop-up celestial globe, cut 2 slightly reduced hexagonal pieces of cardboard and 12 slightly reduced trapezoidal pieces of cardboard to glue individually to the back elements of Figures 1-2a and 1-2b. Glue hemispheres together according to instructions.

Figure 1-2a. Northern hemisphere of pop-up celestial globe.

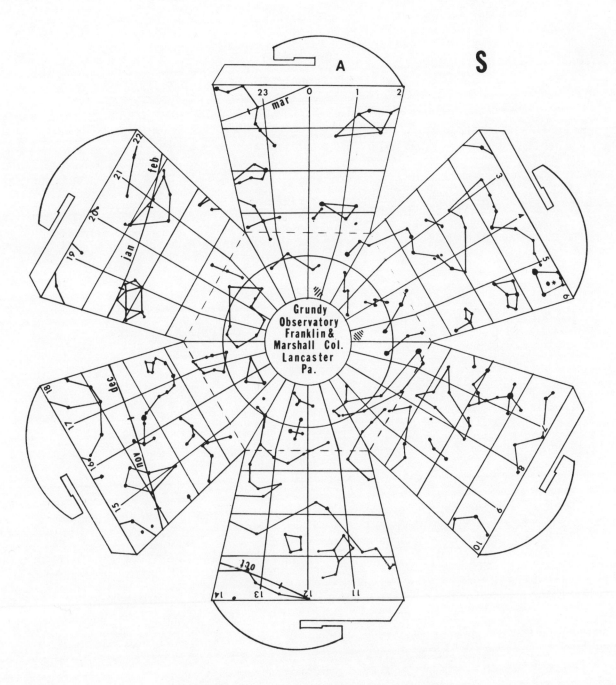

Figure 1-2b. Southern hemisphere of pop-up globe.

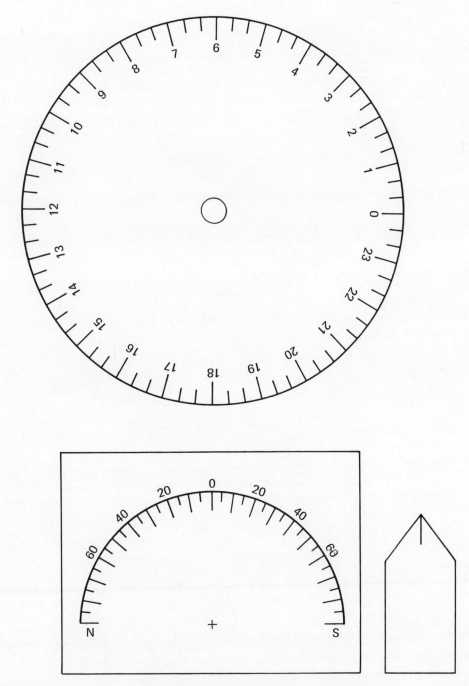

Figure 7-4. Starfinder dials and pointer.

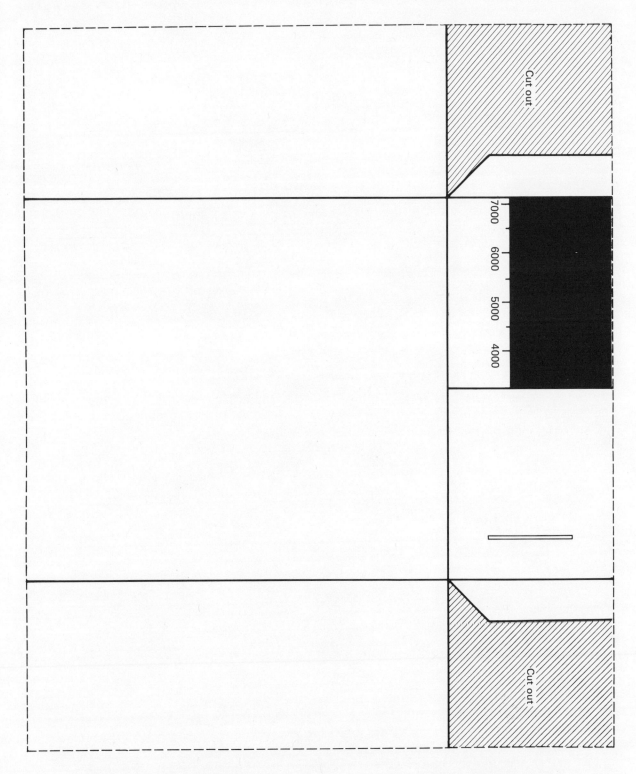

Figure 25-4a. Cut-out for box spectroscope. Cut slit very carefully with razor blade. Glue to Figure 25-4b before folding into box.

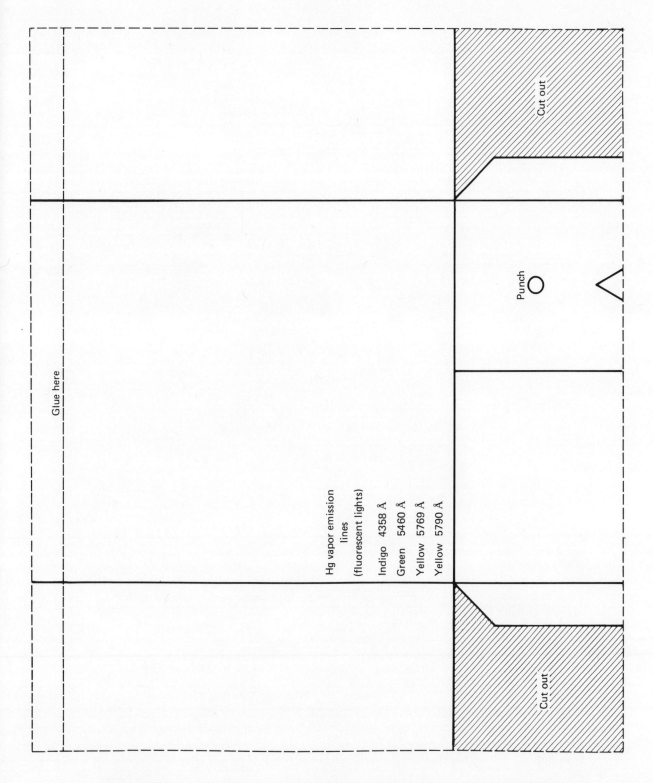

Glue here

Cut out

Punch

Hg vapor emission
lines
(fluorescent lights)

Indigo 4358 Å
Green 5460 Å
Yellow 5769 Å
Yellow 5790 Å

Cut out

Figure 25-4b. Cut-out for box spectroscope. Cut out and glue to Figure 25-4a before folding into box.

Chart 1

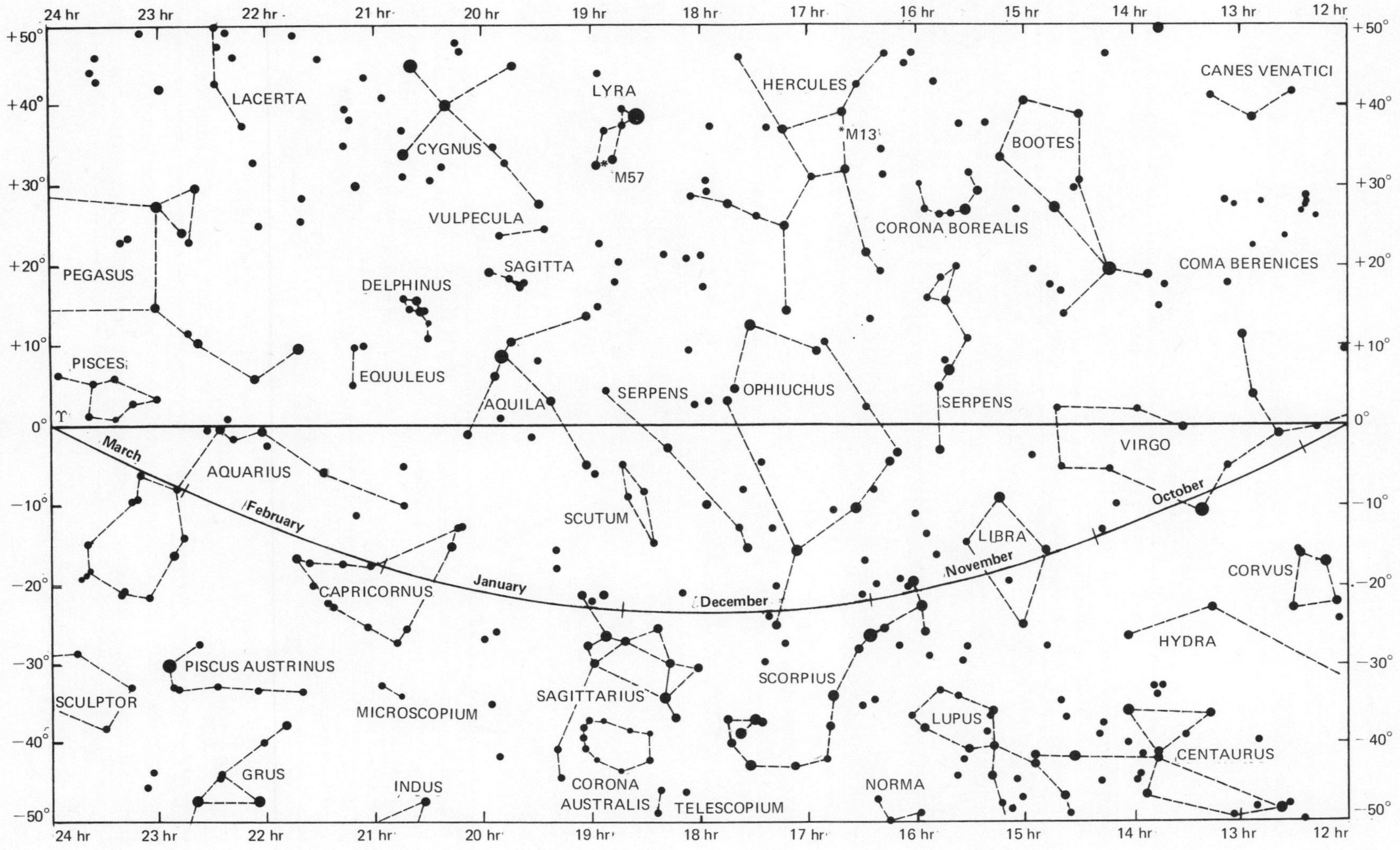

summer sky

287

Chart 2

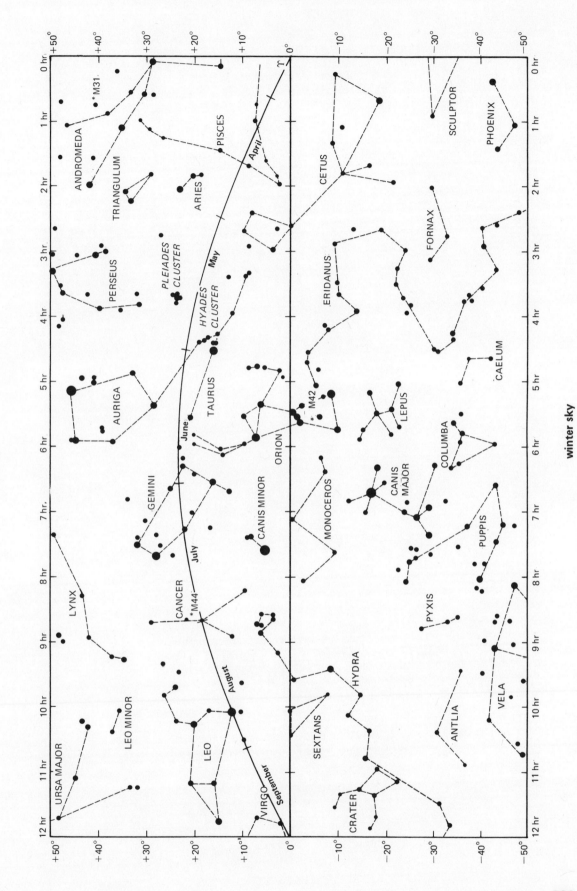

winter sky

Chart 3

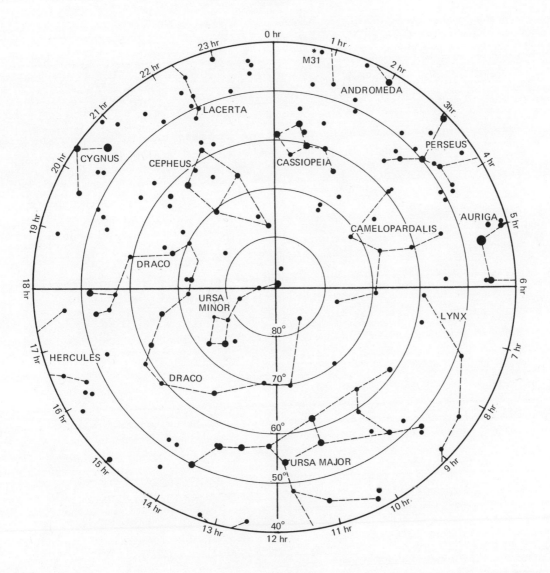

north circumpolar

291